W9-BCU-340

06/24

STAND PRICE
$ 5.00

A WORLD OF LETTERS

A World of Letters

Yale University Press

1908–2008

NICHOLAS A. BASBANES

Yale University Press

NEW HAVEN & LONDON

Published with assistance from the Norman V. Donaldson Memorial Fund
and the foundation established in memory of Philip Hamilton McMillan
of the Class of 1894, Yale College.

Designed by James J. Johnson and set in Adobe Caslon by
Duke & Company, Devon, Pennsylvania.
Printed in the United States of America by Sheridan Books.

Library of Congress Cataloging-in-Publication Data

Basbanes, Nicholas A., 1943–
A world of letters : Yale University Press, 1908–2008 / Nicholas A. Basbanes.
    p.   cm.
Includes bibliographical references.
ISBN 978-0-300-11598-7 (alk. paper)

1. Yale University Press—History. 2. University presses—Connecticut—
New Haven—History—20th century. 3. Scholarly publishing—
Connecticut—New Haven—History—20th century. I. Title.
Z473.Y32B37 2008
070.5'94—dc22   2008017680

A catalogue record for this book is available from the British Library.

This paper meets the requirements of ANSI/NISO Z39.48-1992
(Permanence of Paper). It contains 30 percent postconsumer waste (PCW)
and is certified by the Forest Stewardship Council (FSC).

10 9 8 7 6 5 4 3 2 1

For Constance V. Basbanes

Contents

Illustrations follow pages 80 and 128

Preface

The centennial of Yale University Press comes at a time when scholarly publishers everywhere are considering creative ways to remain viable in the face of what all agree is a "crisis" in the way they have always gone about their business. With the advent in recent years of what we might call the "electronic alternative" to traditional publishing—a development of such unprecedented consequence that the whole notion of book culture is a topic of unending speculation—the role of the university press in the twenty-first century has become a hot topic.

Beyond the long shadow cast by the computer, a good deal of the concern stems from the steady erosion of a core market, with so many academic and research libraries no longer buying books that once came to them routinely on standing order, eliminating what was once a dependable outlet for even the most esoteric of monographs. Added to that trend has been the continued disappearance of the independent bookstore, reduced budgets for the buying of books exacerbated by the skyrocketing cost of scholarly journals, and the growing dominance of online retailers, each a factor that, in its own way, has had a rippling effect on scholarly publishing.

To appreciate the degree of unease that is endemic, one need only read *University Publishing in a Digital Age,* a detailed report released in July 2007 that was prepared collaboratively by Laura Brown, former president of Oxford University Press USA, and Ithaka, a nonprofit research and consulting organization focused on higher education and technology. Described by its authors as a "qualitative review" of material gathered from a survey of American university presses, the report drew also on interviews conducted with press directors, librarians, provosts, and other administrators. Among their findings was evidence that university presses suffer from "a drift" in which they have become "less integrated with the core activities and missions of their home campuses." To combat this disquieting trend, the authors of the report have proposed a joint undertaking that would assume many of the technological and marketing functions that most presses are unable to afford on their own—one that would involve less reliance on traditional bookmaking.

Without naming names, the authors report that "the need for university presses is being questioned at some institutions," with administrators throughout the country "looking to other parts of campus (most commonly libraries) to assume publishing related responsibilities for digital content," while others are reconsidering the way their presses are governed and operated. A good deal of all this anxiety, naturally, is attributed to the "financial stability"—or lack thereof—at so many of the presses, particularly "as demand for their traditional products declines and administrators' appetites for subsidizing them diminish."

To emphasize the latter point, the Ithaka Report noted that of eighty-eight scholarly presses based in American universities, fifty-three responded to the survey, and of these, 72 percent reported that their parent institutions allow them "to operate at a deficit." Given that the thirty-five presses that did not respond to the survey are almost entirely small (the identities of the respondents are listed in an appendix)—and since the Ithaka Report makes clear that "large presses generally are faring better than smaller" ones—it is not a stretch to speculate that the percentage of scholarly presses operating in the red each year is closer to 85 percent.

Taking all of these factors into account, the authors of the report ask the following question: "Ten years from now, how many university presses will be able to compete for authors, or meet the expectations of consumers of scholarly information online, if they only continue what they are doing today?" Their answer—"very few, we expect"—provides the thrust of this prediction: "Publishing in the future will look very different than it has in the past." Describing this as "a pivotal moment," the authors further maintain that "scholarly publishing of the future will need to support content created in new and complex ways, including everything from regularly updated reference material, multimedia projects, and large interlinked centers that add new works regularly, to resources user-generated content."

As bold and as pointed as the Ithaka Report may be—and it is being read carefully throughout the publishing industry—few of its conclusions come as a surprise to anyone who has paid attention to what has been happening over the past couple of decades. It was largely for this reason, in fact, that I welcomed the opportunity to write a history of Yale University Press on its one hundredth birthday. I have been writing about various aspects of books and book culture for thirty years, beginning as the literary editor of a newspaper in Massachusetts, then as a syndicated columnist and freelance writer, and now as the author of seven books to date that have taken in the gamut of this endlessly fascinating world. With that as a stock-in-trade, the offer to enter the life of what I have long regarded as one of the truly outstanding scholarly publishers in the world was irresistible. To have an opportunity to determine how this publisher has managed not only to survive in the face of such formidable obstacles—but to flourish and thrive—seemed a perfect fit.

Because "financial stability," as the authors of the Ithaka Report put it, does matter in scholarly publishing, it is relevant to report that in 2007 Yale University Press finished well in the black, a circumstance that has become an annual expectation at Yale. Although continued fiscal health is impressive, what is especially pertinent are the publishing goals these revenues allow the Press to achieve—the central thrust of this narrative.

"Yale University Press has a special history," one of the many people I interviewed over the past three years for this book told me early on in my research. "We are leading the way toward a new kind of university publishing." Little did I know then how lively the history would be, and how engaging the experiences of the principals. Yet for all the enthusiasm I may profess for what Yale University Press has accomplished, it is important to note that I remain an outsider, and that one of the many inducements I had to take on this project was a commitment from the Press to honor every request for information I might have and to provide access to whatever files or records I wished to examine. It is gratifying to report that every document I requested was furnished, everyone I wanted to interview was made available, and every interview I conducted was helpful and informative. I wish in this regard to express my gratitude to everyone at the Press past and pres-ent who provided so much encouragement and assistance, in particular to John Donatich, John Ryden, Janyce Siress, Laura Jones Dooley, and Sarah Clark, and also to Caroline Kelley, a graduate student whose searches on my behalf in the archives of Sterling Memorial Library during the early months of this project were most helpful.

The motto of Yale University is *lux et veritas*—light and truth—words that have special relevance to a publishing enterprise whose goal it is to create an enduring world of letters. May the next hundred years be equally illuminating, equally enriching.

A WORLD OF LETTERS

ONE

The Formative Decades

HE UNIVERSITY PRESS IS A CURIOUS form of publishing enterprise that has emerged globally by way of two strikingly different sets of circumstances. Certainly the most venerable operations are to be found in the United Kingdom at Oxford and Cambridge Universities, where both institutions maintain publishing enterprises with pedigrees that extend back more than half a millennium, each established around the time that the earliest printing shops were being set up in England by William Caxton and his followers. First to issue a book under its name was Oxford, with the release in 1478 of an obscure commentary on the Apostles' Creed attributed to Jerome; it was printed by Theodoric Rood, a German expatriate credited with producing seventeen titles for the university through 1484. Despite such a fruitful beginning, output there was haphazard and inconsistent at best over the next century,

and production did not become firmly institutionalized until 1586, when the Star Chamber—at the urging of the earl of Leicester, the university chancellor and a favorite of Queen Elizabeth I—granted Oxford a decree confirming its privilege to print books. Thirty-five years later, the university received royal permission to produce and sell the King James Authorized Version of the Bible, an extraordinary concession that assured profitability in the centuries to come and contributed measurably to a long period of sustained growth that would be highlighted by such early efforts as Sir Francis Bacon's *Advancement of Learning* (1605), Captain John Smith's *Map of Virginia* (1612), and Robert Burton's *Anatomy of Melancholy* (1621). The Crown granted similar permission to Cambridge University Press, which had been established in 1521. Before long Cambridge would be publishing the original writings of such luminaries as John Milton, John Dryden, William Harvey, Isaac Newton, James Clerk-Maxwell, and Lord Kelvin, works of lasting literary and scientific significance that set a pattern for generations to come. But it was the steady sale of Bibles, many millions of them over the decades, that assured financial stability for both imprints and made possible the steady publication of other worthy efforts that continue to distinguish their names and bring credit to their parent institutions.

In the New World, as with everything else, the historical record is far more truncated than the European example, with the American form of academic press emerging in the late nineteenth and early twentieth centuries as a response to the professionalization of scholarship then taking place throughout the United States and Canada, and as a way to document the pioneering work being produced. Two of the earliest endeavors to begin operations in North America did so as deliberate components of newly established research institutions. The Johns Hopkins University Press—the oldest university press in continuous operation in the United States—was formed in 1878, just two years after the institution itself opened under the leadership of Daniel Coit Gilman, an imaginative educator who famously declared that one of the "noblest duties" of a university is to "advance knowledge and to diffuse it not merely among those who can attend the daily lectures—but far and wide." When that bold statement of purpose was proclaimed, the promulgation of ideas to points "far and wide" meant intellectual enrichment by means of the printed word. Gilman's point, made simply, was that if ideas and discoveries were to be shared, they had to appear first between the hard covers of bound books or as articles and essays in reputable journals, a conviction he nurtured during his nine-year tenure (1856–1865) as college librarian and professor of physical and political geography at Yale, where he received his bachelor's degree in 1852, and as president of the University of California from 1872 to 1875.

A similar dynamic took place at the University of Chicago, an institution established in 1890 by John D. Rockefeller with a clear mandate to stimulate probing inquiry among a new generation of carefully trained scholars. Like Johns Hopkins, this new center of learning was conceived as a nexus of primary research that would develop specialized graduate programs then unheard of in the United States but common in Europe. William Rainey Harper, the founding president, was a brilliant strategist whose innovative approach was to combine the interdisciplinary strength of American liberal arts colleges with the rigorous structure of German research universities. An essential element of success, he made clear, was the immediate organization of a publishing unit that would be an "organic part of the institution," not an "incident" or informal "attachment" to the overall scheme. The formation of a press was included in his original plans for the university, created, in fact, as one of four major divisions, to be controlled by a special committee of trustees but operated as a private corporation. Harper's strategy paid immediate dividends; by 1900, the press had published 127 books and pamphlets and set up eleven scholarly journals featuring original contributions in education, the social sciences, the humanities, and the physical sciences. In 1907, Albert A. Michelson, a University of Chicago physicist credited with determining the speed of light, became the first American scientist to receive a Nobel Prize; the books outlining many of his findings—*The Velocity of Light* (1902), *Light Waves and Their Uses* (1903), and *Studies in Optics* (1927)— were published by the University of Chicago Press, which today claims twenty Nobel laureates among its authors.

Rounding out the first generation of North American

academic presses were the University of California and Columbia University, which both established publishing divisions in 1893, followed by the University of Toronto in 1901. In the early years of the twentieth century, the founding spirit at Columbia, Nicholas Murray Butler—philosopher, diplomat, winner in 1931 of a Nobel Peace Prize, and from 1902 to 1945 president of both the university he transformed and the press he urged into being to serve it—had expressed repeated concern that "marked activity" in the production of original research being done on the Morningside Heights campus was not reaching a broad audience because such "contributions to knowledge are always of a technical character and usually destitute of commercial value." The only alternative, he felt, was to set up a publishing unit that would support the massive expansion in advanced educational programs he was introducing at Columbia and ensure that the product of these pursuits was disseminated widely.

In 1905, the New York publisher Charles Scribner, Princeton Class of 1875 and a Princeton trustee, took the initiative to get a publishing operation up and running at his alma mater. Scribner had been toying with ways to go about publishing scholarly monographs not feasible for commercial ventures when he was presented with a proposal to support an independent academic press. In addition to furnishing seed money, Scribner bought the land for the headquarters, furnished it with printing equipment, and underwrote construction of a building designed by his brother-in-law, the architect Ernest Flagg.

His ideal for the press, according to an editorial in the *New York Herald Tribune*, was to promote "disinterested service to Literature." Incorporated as a self-supporting corporation to be operated apart from the university—an arrangement that continues there to this day—Princeton University Press would publish nearly four hundred books in its first twenty years and provide the conceptual model for three enterprising Yale graduates who were intent on establishing a nonprofit publishing enterprise of their own a few years later.

The Yale trio included George Parmly Day, Class of 1897, and his older brother, Clarence S. Day, Jr., Class of 1896, the sons of Clarence Shepard Day, Sr., Class of 1876, a prominent New York broker, banker, railroad director, and for many years governor of the New York Stock Exchange; they were also the grandsons of Benjamin Henry Day, the founder of the *New York Sun*, and the nephews of Benjamin Day, the inventor in 1879 of an engraving process used in commercial printing to add shading, texture, and tone to images that continues to bear the name Benday. In 1907, the Day brothers received the blessing of Yale president Arthur Twining Hadley to organize what they modestly chose to call the Yale Publishing Association and to take operational control of the *Yale Alumni Weekly*; they also introduced a scholarly quarterly, the *Yale Review*, that in time would achieve world renown and by midcentury operate on its own. Joining them in their modest undertaking was a classmate of Clarence's, Edwin Oviatt, who would edit the alumni weekly and later write an institutional history published by the Press in 1916, *The Beginnings of Yale (1701–1726)*. Their careful effort to publish *The Journal of an Expedition across Venezuela and Columbia* by Yale professor Hiram Bingham—an accomplished explorer soon to be acclaimed as the discoverer of Machu Picchu and later to serve as a United States senator from Connecticut—increased their standing with President Hadley, who in 1908 allowed them to call their enterprise Yale University Press, with the explicit understanding that the university would monitor its activities. In 1919, as Hadley reflected on his two decades as Yale president, he deemed the *Yale Review* and Yale University Press to have been "our best products of the past twenty years."

Sickly for much of his adult life—he died in 1935 at age sixty-one—Clarence Day, Jr., achieved celebrity as an author, most famously of a best-selling memoir of growing up in Manhattan in the 1890s as one of four sons in an affluent East Side household headed by a domineering father. Published five months before his death, *Life with Father* became the basis of a comedy adapted for the stage by Howard Lindsay and Russel Crouse. It opened on Broadway in 1939 and ran for a record 3,224 performances; a 1947 film starring William Powell, Irene Dunne, and a very young Elizabeth Taylor received Oscar nominations for cinematography, art direction, musical score, and best actor.

Apart from lending his full enthusiasm to the Press, Clarence Day was content to allow his younger brother be the prime mover in the ambitious initiative, which began operations not in New Haven but in New York, where George Parmly Day was gainfully employed in his father's Wall Street brokerage firm and in no position, just yet, to give up his day job. The enterprise briefly set up its headquarters in what he described years later as a "ten by twelve" room before moving into a marginally larger space—"a little black cave" of an office—in the Ginn Building at 70 Fifth Avenue near Washington Square. The workforce during that embryonic period consisted entirely of George Day's wife, Wilhelmine Octavia Johnson Day, who was responsible for keeping a record of all the Press's work "in a ridiculous book, four by seven, with a thin cover that looked like butchers' paper," according to a charming reminiscence written by Clarence Day, Jr., in 1920. Each morning, Clarence Day recalled in the chatty piece, Wilhelmine "rushed" to the front door of the building to see if the postman "had shoved any mail through the slot of the door; and when some of it was orders she had to telephone downtown at once to announce them, because orders make you happy when you are starting a publishing business. One morning there was a splendid order for thirty-one books, and it took her all day to get them tied up and sent off and billed for."

Long after a full-time staff was in place handling Press affairs in New Haven, Wilhelmine Day retained an abiding interest in its well-being. An orphan raised by a guardian, and childless throughout her fifty-seven-year marriage to George Parmly Day, she was a formidable presence, and not shy about offering an opinion. Such was the case in 1931, when she returned from a trip to Europe and urged her husband to publish an overview of economic reform then being attempted in Sweden as a response to world depression, an experiment in government that would later be described as a "constructive compromise between capitalism and socialism." Following her advice, the Press commissioned Marquis W. Childs, a young foreign correspondent for the *St. Louis Post-Dispatch* who had reported from Stockholm, to write *Sweden: The Middle Way,* which in 1936 became an international best seller, so influential that Yale published a sequel, *Sweden: The Middle Way on Trial,* forty-four years later. Alvin Eisenman, founder and director of the graphic design program at the Yale School of Art and one in a long line of great printers and graphic designers to work at the Press, told Roberta Yerkes Blanshard, an editorial employee from 1929 to 1950, about a telephone call he received from the boss's wife on his first day of employment as a Yale typographer in 1951. "Mr. Eisenman," she told him, "I want you to know that Mr. Day and I never had any children. The Yale Press is our child, and I want you to treat it carefully." At that point, according to Eisenman, "Click, she hung up. And never mentioned it again."

Clarence Day's good-natured essay "The Story of the Yale University Press Told by a Friend" reflected lightly on the first dozen years of the bold publishing project he had undertaken with his brother and was written with the idea that it might persuade prospective donors to help the operation secure financial stability beyond what they were able to commit themselves, and—while they were at it—underwrite the establishment of a printing plant of its own. Day noted how Yale's sibling press at Princeton already had "a beautiful plant, which was given [to] it by Mr. Charles Scribner," presented by the New York publisher in the spirit of builders who "enjoy watching their work grow, and get some fun out of giving." Day used the metaphor of a builder repeatedly in his piece, most pointedly to describe the process of making worthwhile books. "The publisher who thinks of himself as a builder of ships, will naturally care about designing and building them well. The types and the paper and the bindings must be stately and strong—or have whatever characteristics suit the contents and life of each volume." What he was saying, in essence, was that if Yale were to achieve true excellence as an academic publisher, an onsite plant was essential to ensure that "beauty of workmanship and design" would always come first, and that "the object would be to make each book perfect if possible. Not books de luxe only, but every kind, each in its way."

Yale University Press would indeed open a printing office at 119 Wall Street in New Haven—the fourth of seven locations the Press called home over its first century—and manufacture its books before finally finding it more economically prudent in 1973 to farm the work out to subcontractors while maintaining strict supervision over design and layout. By far the most enduring legacy of Clarence Day's clarion call to "make each book perfect" as a physical object is an unbending commitment to production and aesthetics that has distinguished books bearing the YUP imprint from the outset of its existence, and which continues to this day. From 1918 to 1948, every book published by Yale was designed under the supervision of University Printer Carl Purington Rollins, a craftsman of many talents whose contributions to the book arts have been widely celebrated, in one year alone by the American Institute of Graphic Arts and the Grolier Club of New York, which in 1949 jointly mounted a selective exhibition of his work, and by Sterling Memorial Library at Yale, which in 1993 put on a comprehensive retrospective of its own, "Printing at Yale: The Legacy of Carl Purington Rollins." Over a thirty-year period, fifty-nine of Rollins's books were selected by the American Institute of Graphic Arts for representation in its annual exhibition of the finest books published during the preceding twelve months. An article in the January 1928 issue of the periodical *American Collector* by the writer Vrest Orton credited Rollins with having successfully labored to "recover the technique of hand set type, taking into account the machine and modern conditions. He has had the opportunity to effect, in these few years, an absolute turnover of all printing standards and styles that formerly held there." His most important contribution, Orton wrote, was "to take the spirit and the practices of the printers of other times and to work them out with modern tools under modern conditions." In *The Printed Book in America,* a landmark study of American bookmaking published in 1977, Joseph Blumenthal called Rollins an "excellent designer" whose typography "was solid, mature, and pleasing, with strength and sensitivity. . . . His profound respect for literature evoked a logical and forthright clarity in his handling of type. In upholding these typographic virtues and making them evident, Rollins' impact was wide and clear, especially on the many university presses from coast to coast that became a vital force in American publishing. The high standards of bookmaking maintained by these learned presses bear a large measure of debt to the inspiration of Carl Rollins."

But in 1920, when Clarence Day was issuing his appeal to donors, these achievements lay well in the future, and he underscored his buoyant remarks with a stirring statement of purpose that has been reproduced and hung on the walls of numerous publishing houses over the years and turns up often during Google searches for appealing quotations on the primacy of books as civilizing tools. "The world of books is the most remarkable creation of man," he declared. "Nothing else that he builds ever lasts. Monuments fall; nations perish; civilizations grow old and die out; and, after an era of darkness, new races build others. But in the world of books are volumes that have seen this happen again and again, and yet live on, still young, still as fresh as the day they were written, still telling men's hearts of the hearts of men centuries dead."

Yale University Press, for its part, was determined to participate in that noble effort, and wasted little time acquiring important works of scholarship to publish under its standard. Issued in 1909, *The Beginnings of Gospel Story: A*

Historico-Critical Inquiry into the Sources and Structure of the Gospel according to Mark, with Expository Notes upon the Text, for English Readers, by Benjamin W. Bacon, a professor of New Testament criticism and interpretation at the Yale Divinity School, holds the distinction of being the first title to bear the imprint of Yale University Press. Other scholarly monographs followed in due course, including the first installments in what would become a distinguished series of original works in the humanities, Yale Studies in English.

In 1910, George Parmly Day was appointed treasurer of Yale University, and he promptly moved from New York to New Haven. The Press of course traveled with him and operated under his direct control for the next thirty-two years, and in his shadow until 1959, when he died at the age of eighty-three. In 1913, Day published the first installment of the historian Max Farrand's *Records of the Federal Convention of 1787,* an exhaustive work in three volumes that is still regarded as one of the great documentary works of the early twentieth century. In an Alumni Day address given the following year titled "The New Era in Publishing at Yale," the young publisher was pleased to report that his press had issued 125 titles during its first five years of operation. He commended the few book projects that had preceded his initiative, mainly the occasional publication by various individuals of endowed lectures delivered on campus, calling them "significant of the vision of a few men that they might serve the world of scholarship." But those earlier efforts, he asserted, "did not testify—as a University

Press inevitably testifies—to a real awakening on the part of the whole University to its opportunity to disseminate knowledge, to spread truth and light, far beyond its own walls, not merely from time to time, but all the time. They could not give—as a University Press must tend to give—added enthusiasm to research in the University through the confidence felt by the worker that his labors will not be deprived of their proper reward, adequate and timely publication, and will not be nullified because there is no provision for such publication in a year's University budget."

Some eighteen hundred titles were issued during the George Parmly Day era, and they set the tone for a comprehensive approach to academic publishing that placed a premium on solid scholarship and elegant presentation. In 1935, the Press won its first Pulitzer Prize, awarded to Charles McLean Andrews, a retired history professor at the university and editor of the Yale Historical Series, for *The Colonial Period of American History,* the first installment in a four-volume work. Yale has had its share, too, of grand publishing projects that were decades in the making, including one started in 1954 as a joint venture with the American Philosophical Society to publish the vast oeuvre of papers, correspondence, and writings of Benjamin Franklin, an exhaustive scholarly effort that proceeds forward methodically to this day after more than half a century of operations. Ellen R. Cohn, general editor and director of the Franklin Papers, expects that the forty-seventh and final volume in the series will be completed sometime in the next decade (the thirty-eighth installment appeared in November 2006, and the thirty-ninth was scheduled for publication in January 2009). Funding for the program has been provided by a number of benefactors, on the governmental level by the National Endowment for the Humanities and the National Historical Publications and Records Commission, and privately by the Packard Humanities Institute through Founding Fathers Papers, Inc., the Florence Gould Foundation, The Barkley Fund, and The Pew Charitable Trusts.

If the final number of volumes issued in the Franklin Papers series is, indeed, forty-seven, then it will be one fewer than the forty-eight-volume effort produced by the Press between 1924 and 1982 in what is known as *The Yale Edition of Horace Walpole's Correspondence*. Unlike the Franklin Papers, which has been supported by a variety of public and private benefactors, the Walpole correspondence was totally underwritten by a 1918 Yale graduate who spent his entire adult life collecting everything he could find pertaining to the eighteenth-century English writer Horace Walpole, and committing a good portion of his personal fortune to get what he had gathered published in a uniform edition by his alma mater. Wilmarth Sheldon "Lefty" Lewis acquired material with such determination that he is said to have outbid his own agent at a New York auction for a keenly coveted item, his consuming zeal for the chase of sufficient interest that it occasioned the writing of a two-part profile in the *New Yorker* by Geoffrey T. Hellman (August 6 and 13, 1949). Hellman described Lewis in the first essay as a man with "chiseled features, English clothes, an authoritative air, an inquiring, skeptical eye, a cultivated and witty conversational style, a collector's mania, a flawless worldly charm, independent means, and a strong sense of scholarship."

It was the "independent means," of course, that had made everything possible; Lewis's wife, Annie Burr Auchincloss Lewis, was a granddaughter of Oliver B. Jennings, one of the founders of the Standard Oil Company, and pleased to devote a good deal of the family fortune to fulfilling her husband's unbridled pursuit. At his death in 1979 at eighty-three, Lewis—by that time a widower with no immediate survivors—left his magnificent home in Farmington, Connecticut, and his Walpole collection to Yale, where he had been a trustee for twenty-five years and a valued friend of the Press as well. Lewis also provided sufficient funds to complete *The Yale Edition of Horace Walpole's Correspondence*, which issued its final installment three years later. Shortly after the series had been completed, Warren Hunting Smith, an editor who spent five decades toiling in Sterling Library on the project, talked with Mel Gussow of the *New York Times*, describing it as a unique experience. "It was something like existing in a monastery," he said. "There were these Gothic arches, and we were sitting there like medieval monks, reading manuscripts." He told how pleasant it had been working peacefully in "the backwater of the university" all that time, toiling away in what was known around the university as the Walpole Factory.

Another long-term effort of special note was the *Bibliography of American Literature*, a comprehensive reference in nine volumes published between 1955 and 1991 that describes nearly forty thousand literary works of approximately three hundred American writers from the time of the American Revolution to 1930, published by the Press for the Bibliographical Society of America and begun under the general editorship of Jacob Blanck, at one time the bibliographer of Americana for the Library of Congress. Blanck compiled the basic data for all of the volumes and saw volumes 1 to 6 through to publication; after his death in 1974, volume 7 was completed and edited for publication by Virginia L. Smyers and Michael Winship, volumes 8 and 9 by Michael Winship alone. Renowned for the accuracy and extent of its publication details—the entries list every reprint and variant edition of an author's works, including obscure and fugitive appearances in anthologies, broadsides, and gift books, and list details on bindings and physical features of the various editions—the stout folios are regarded by librarians, booksellers, and collectors as indispensable, and generally referred to by them simply as *BAL*.

Other important series in literature, history, economics, and language were launched that drew on faculty strengths. Chief among them: *The Yale Edition of the Works of Samuel Johnson*, a half-century project begun in 1955 that has to date produced eighteen volumes; *The Works of Jonathan Edwards*, a twenty-six-volume series begun in 1957 and completed in 2008 of sermons and writings of a major eighteenth-century theologian, philosopher, missionary to Native Americans, and Yale graduate; the Yale Judaica Series, a comprehensive series of translations of ancient and medieval Jewish classics from Hebrew, Aramaic, Ethiopic, and Arabic, including fourteen volumes of *The Code of Maimonides*.

Of particular merit as well is *The Yale Edition of the Complete Works of St. Thomas More*, a fifteen-volume project begun in 1963 and completed in 1997 under the guidance of Louis L. Martz of the Yale English Department, whose contributions to the Press and its scholarly output in general were many throughout a career that spanned four decades. In addition to a productive membership on the Publications Committee, Martz wrote or edited twenty-five books, including several written for Yale, notably *The Poetry of Meditation: A Study in English Religious Literature of the Seventeenth Century* (1954), *The Paradise Within: Studies in Vaughan, Traherne, and Milton* (1964), and *Poet of Exile: A Study of Milton's Poetry* (1980). At his death in 2002 at the age of eighty-eight, Martz was praised by his colleague professor emeritus Dwight Culler as "one of the most distinguished figures in the Yale English Department during what many would call the 'glory days' of the 1950s to the 1970s." Along with Cleanth Brooks and Maynard Mack, Culler added, Martz "moved the English Department from a purely historical study of literature through the New Criticism to a broader humanistic and religious concern."

Another publishing program undertaken in tandem with the English Department, the Yale Shakespeare (known over

time around the Press by the acronym TYS), was established
in 1917 with a fifty-thousand-dollar grant from the Kingsley
Trust Association, also known as the Scroll and Key Society
of Yale College, with two prominent members of the faculty,
Wilbur L. Cross and Tucker Brooke, named as general editors. A native of Mansfield, Connecticut, and a Yale man to
the core—B.A. 1885, Ph.D. 1889—Professor Cross had already
been recruited by George Parmly Day to edit the *Yale Review*, a voluntary task he performed from 1911 to 1940. After
relinquishing his formal duties at the university in 1930 at the
mandatory retirement age of sixty-eight—his various positions had included Sterling Professor of English, university
provost, and dean of the Graduate School—Cross decided to
run for governor of Connecticut as a Democrat in what was
then a staunchly Republican state; that November he won
what would be the first of four two-year terms, holding office
from 1931 to 1939. His colleague on the Shakespeare project,
Tucker Brooke, was a Rhodes Scholar from West Virginia
who earned two degrees from Oxford University and enjoyed
great renown on both sides of the Atlantic as an authority
on Elizabethan literature. To help them edit the individual
volumes, Cross and Brooke enlisted colleagues in the English Department, making the project a true Yale production,
a point proudly made on the half-title page of every copy
printed in the series: "Published under the direction of the
Department of English, Yale University, on the fund given
to the Yale University Press in 1917 by the members of the

Kingsley Trust Association (Scroll and Key Society of Yale College) to commemorate the seventy-fifth anniversary of the founding of the society."

Between 1918 and 1929, all the plays attributed to Shakespeare were issued in compact, hardcover editions, usually in batches of three or four volumes a year; they were reprinted numerous times over the next decade, then brought out again in the 1940s and 1950s in revised editions. Each of the forty volumes issued—one for each of the thirty-seven plays, plus others for the poems, sonnets, and a short biography—included a brief introduction, an index, and an apparatus quite new for the period, the addition of brief glosses at the foot of most pages to illuminate words, phrases, and quaint concepts that might be unfamiliar to a contemporary readership. Though decidedly dated and obsolete by today's scholarly standards, the books were enormously popular in classrooms throughout the English-speaking world, and affordably priced at fifty cents a volume. The appeal of the series was such that a single-volume edition was offered by the Book-of-the-Month Club as an alternate selection during the 1960s.

"For its era, it tried to be a relatively uncluttered text, which was good for the times, and it made the text quite readable," is how Burton Raffel, editor for Yale of the Annotated Shakespeare, a new series launched in 2003, assessed the earlier effort for me. But from the Press's standpoint, even more significant was the contribution the Yale Shakespeare made toward balancing the operating budget. "It was the most influential, significant, and widely known of anything that appeared under the Yale imprint—and the only one that bore the name of both the Press and the university," John G. Ryden, director of the Press from 1979 to 2002, told me. "It wouldn't be much of an exaggeration to say that TYS bears much the same relation to Yale as the Bible did to the presses at Oxford and Cambridge. It was the most enduring publication of the first fifty years." Ryden said he was told early on in his twenty-three-year tenure in New Haven that the Yale Shakespeare—and another series that was enormously popular during the George Parmly Day era known as the Chronicles of America—"kept the Press alive during the Depression."

The Chronicles of America were compact, profusely illustrated, one-volume histories issued ten titles at a time between 1917 and 1922, each focusing on a specific event, theme, or individual in American history and written by prominent historians. The idea for the series was proposed to Yale by Robert Glasgow, a self-made Toronto publisher who between 1914 and 1917 had marshaled into print a twenty-three-volume Canada and Its Provinces series and a thirty-volume Chronicles of Canada series, both hugely successful and highly regarded efforts that had integrated the contributions of dozens of writers. The texts for the Chronicles of America were prepared under the supervision of Allen Johnson, a professor of history at Yale who served as general editor. Before taking on the assignment, Johnson had written several important books, among them *Stephen A. Douglas: A Study in American*

Politics (1908) and *Readings in American Constitutional History, 1776–1876* (1912); he would later be hired by the American Council of Learned Societies to serve as general editor of the *Dictionary of American Biography* (*DAB*), published by Scribner's between 1928 and 1936.

Because the chronicles were released in groups of ten, they tended to be reviewed summarily, albeit favorably. "The same high standard of scholarship and excellent simplicity of style characteristic of the first ten volumes of *The Chronicles of America* are present also in the second installment in the series," the *New York Times* observed on May 14, 1919. "The books are not encumbered by footnotes, their form is beautiful, the aim is always to tell a story, interesting for its own sake." When ten more volumes came out the following year, the *Times* was calling the chronicles a "monumental" effort and applauded them for "their freshness, their readability, their freedom from pedantry." When the Press issued its fifth and final batch in 1922, the newspaper expressed particular pleasure that an account of Woodrow Wilson's performance in the recently completed world war written by Charles Seymour and a concise consideration of Theodore Roosevelt and his times by Howard Howland were among the new efforts to be released. "The method makes for freshness and variety of treatment and for ease and comfort of use by busy people, since the whole history can thus be read in small installments at odd moments."

Three months after the final ten volumes were issued, Glasgow died of a heart attack in New York at the age of

forty-six. On September 27, 1923—just five months after
Glasgow's death—George Parmly Day announced the "dawn
of a new day for motion pictures" with the forthcoming release
of a series of silent films then being produced jointly by the
Press and an enterprise formed two years earlier known as the
Chronicles of America Picture Corporation, of which he was
the president. The fully staged films, which would be known
collectively as the Chronicles of America Photoplays, were
being made, Day said, with a goal of "making the motion picture theatres a powerful agency for good in each community,"
and he called on "every citizen to support by his patronage,
and to encourage others to support, photoplays of the highest type, thus encouraging producers and exhibitors to devote
their energies and resources to these in preference to others."
Underlying this hopeful call was a concern Day obviously
had for what was then being shown about the land in a wildly
successful entertainment medium that some people felt—in
an argument that resonates today in the age of computers and
the Internet—would lead to a decline in reading among young
people. "If the motion pictures shown in its theatres, as well
as in its schools, are of a high standard of excellence," Day
reasoned, "no community need fear the influence undoubtedly and most effectively exercised by the movies." To raise
private capital to fund the boldly ambitious enterprise, stock
had been sold at sixty dollars a share.

Yet with the unexpected death of Glasgow—he had
been vice president of the Chronicles of America Picture

Corporation, and the person responsible for making the films—concern soon arose at the Press that the adaptations being written by the theatrical writers he had hired were taking liberties with the factual record. To ensure that Yale's interests would be protected, the historian Max Farrand was named project editor; another faculty member, Frank Ellsworth Spaulding, head of the Department of Education, and the historian Nathaniel Wright Stephenson, author of three books in the chronicles series and a visiting professor at Yale, came on board to assist as principal advisers. Other historians consulted included Charles McLean Andrews of Yale, Joseph Schafer of the State Historical Society of Wisconsin, and Edgar Robinson of Stanford University. When Arthur Brook, treasurer of the Chronicles of America Picture Corporation and Glasgow's business partner, agreed to give full textual authority to the "scholars in all matters of content," filming proceeded, though not without complications.

In a memorandum written to a colleague during production, Stephenson—who became the "guiding light of the Photoplays series" for Yale, according to historian Ian R. Tyrrell—complained about the script writers they were working with by asking a question clearly born of frustration: "Must we conclude that some people who have not thought much in historical terms do not form the same mental pictures which we do when we talk with them about historical forces?" On the production side, there was similar annoyance. Arthur E. Krows, one of Glasgow's original associates in the venture, and secretary of the corporation, resigned when Stephenson demanded that he make changes in the scripts for the first two films, *Columbus* and *Jamestown*. Years later, Krows would write a series of angry reminiscences for a trade magazine about these experiences that singled out a group of unnamed "professors" and "alleged experts" whose "meddling" had been responsible for causing long delays on film sets and for production costs that had spiraled out of control. Very little time passed, he wrote, before "word spread throughout the theatrical district that here was a fine, fat, foolish cow waiting to be milked, and players and technical men flocked without conscience to share the cream." The level of "historical authenticity" that had been demanded by the editors, however, was described approvingly by the Metropolitan Museum of Art, which reported in its official bulletin the "pleasure" its staff felt in having been "one of the first institutions to obtain" the films for educational use: "What sort of fences did George Washington jump over when he went hunting in Virginia? What kind of a hunting horn did he use? What books might have been in Wolfe's cabin when he sailed across to capture Quebec? Was there moonlight on the night of a particular battle of the Mexican War? And how were the tails of the soldiers' horses cut? Countless such tiny matters, as well as the accuracy of the central action, have received the careful attention of the Chronicles' own special research workers."

The original plan had called for the making of forty films but was scaled back to thirty-three. In the end, fifteen productions, each consisting of three fifteen-minute reels, were released in 1923 and 1924 bearing such titles as *The Pilgrims, Peter Stuyvesant, The Gateway to the West, Alexander Hamilton, The Declaration of Independence, Yorktown, Dixie,* and *The Frontier Woman.* Day's idea had been to lease the films to boards of education and private schools throughout the country and give them free of charge to rural districts, but because fewer than half of the films were ever made, the venture, according to a 1926 article in *Time* magazine, "was found financially impracticable," and by 1930, stock in the corporation had fallen to ten dollars a share. In 1933, George Parmly Day wrote a gloomy letter to shareholders advising them not to expect any dividends soon. "Despite the admitted excellence of the fifteen *Chronicles of America Photoplays,*" he wrote, "the revenue from their theatrical distribution, has, in view of the lack of cooperation from the industry, never been large and is now merely nominal." The films remained available into the 1950s, but demand for them was sparse—the age of sound in films introduced in 1929 had rendered these silent efforts quaintly obsolete—and the corporation was finally dissolved in 1960.

Yale's fling in the movie business had come to an end, but not without some effort at self-analysis, at least in terms of the impact the films might have had on the intended audience. In 1929, the Press published the results of research it had commissioned by two Yale professors, Daniel Chauncey Knowlton and John Warren Tilton of the Department of Education, to "measure the contribution of the photoplays to enrichment, retention, and the creation of interest" on youngsters who viewed them in classroom settings. Their study was conducted among students in the Troup Junior High School in New Haven, the results were reported in *Motion Pictures in History Teaching: A Study of the Chronicles of America, as an Aid in Seventh Grade Instruction.* Among the findings: "That the photoplays contributed materially to the gaining and retention of worth-while knowledge," that "they produced more pupil participation in classroom discussion," and "that they caused the pupils who saw them to read voluntarily more supplementary history reading material under controlled classroom settings."

A number of studies have been written about this episode in film history, with the consensus view that this ambitious effort fell short for a number of critical reasons. In an excellent essay for the *Historian,* University of Massachusetts professor Donald J. Mattheisen wrote that the Yale educators "were not small-minded antiquarians who were slavishly preoccupied with details of architecture or dress. They were gifted and intelligent men who mistakenly thought that they could easily master the new medium of film. Their inability to do so seems partly due to the rigid program prescribed by Yale's editors, when the original intention was to translate portions of the *Chronicles* book series into film. The editors tried to do that too literally by stipulating an academic theme and even which events were to be depicted in each film. Their prescriptions created impediments that sometimes forced the films to deal too fleetingly with complex issues. The result was artistic and pedagogic failure."

If there was one overriding lesson to be learned above all others from this unfortunate and ill-considered episode, it was that a university press is well advised to stick with what it does best, which is to seek out and publish solid, relevant, and enduringly important books of demonstrable scholarly merit. Another initiative launched during the early years of the George Parmly Day era, the Yale Series of Younger Poets, is a perfect example of where the Press kept its "eye on the ball," to borrow a phrase from the sports world, and fulfilled its mission nobly by inaugurating—and sustaining now through eighty-nine years—a program of singular distinction that is without equal in the United States. Inaugurated in 1919 as a way to "afford a public medium for the work of young men and women who have not yet secured a wide public recognition," the series is committed to publishing "first books" of poetry, and over nine decades has introduced the work of such artists as James Agee, John Ashbery, Reuel Denney, Paul Engle, Carolyn Forché, Robert Haas, John Hollander, William Meredith, W. S. Merwin, Ted Olson, Adrienne Rich, Norman Rosten, Muriel Rukeyser, George Starbuck, James Tate, and Margaret Walker. One of four Pulitzer Prizes won by the Press over the past hundred years was awarded to the 1961 Younger Poet, Alan Dugan, for his volume *Poems*, which also received a National Book Award. In 2000, Davis McCombs's *Ultima Thule* was a finalist for the National Book Critics Circle Award. Judges over the years have included William Alexander Percy, Stephen Vincent Benét, Archibald MacLeish, W. H. Auden, Stanley Kunitz, James Merrill, James Dickey, and Louise Glück. As many as eight hundred entries are submitted for consideration in a typical year, with the winning submission being assured of publication by the Press. How many copies may or may not be sold is irrelevant; the books are published, new voices are introduced, and many others are encouraged and given hope.

A number of individual titles issued during the George Parmly Day years began life as the texts of addresses delivered at Yale as part of endowed annual programs, best known among them the Terry Lectureship, a series established in 1905 with a gift from Dwight H. Terry, a resident of Bridgeport, Connecticut. Each year, a distinguished scholar is invited to address issues concerning the ways in which science and philosophy inform religion, and to consider the application of religion to human welfare. The speaker is asked to give four lectures over a two-week period, with an edited version of his or her remarks issued by the Press as soon thereafter as feasible. The series has provided a stimulating forum for a rich diversity of incisive discourse, and a number of the books have endured as twentieth-century classics, the following among them:

The Heavenly City of the Eighteenth-Century Philosophers (1932), by Carl Becker, a "rare work of scholarship," according to Peter Gay in a silver-anniversary tribute to the Cornell University historian, "that is also a work of literature—a masterpiece of persuasion that has done more to shape the current image of the Enlightenment than any other book"; *A Common Faith* (1934), the American philosopher John Dewey's proposal for a model of spiritual belief that is not confined to sect, class, or race; *Psychology and Religion* (1938), in which Carl Gustav Jung described what he regarded as an authentic religious function in the unconscious mind, named a Book of the Century by the New York Public Library; *The Meaning of Evolution* (1949), by the paleontologist George Gaylord Simpson, hailed by reviewer Bernard Mishkin in the *New York Times* as being, "without question, the best general work on the meaning of evolution to appear in our time"; *The American Mind: An Interpretation of American Thought and Character since the 1880's* (1950), an incisive examination of American thought and intellectual life at midcentury by the historian Henry Steele Commager; *Psychoanalysis and Religion* (1950), the third work by the world-renowned psychoanalyst and humanist philosopher Erich Fromm; *The Courage to Be* (1952), a seminal work of twentieth-century existential philosophy by the theologian Paul Tillich; and *Becoming* (1955), a far-reaching study of the development of human personality that stressed the importance of self and the uniqueness of adult personality, by the American psychologist Gordon W. Allport.

An even older series, the Silliman Memorial Lecture, was established in 1901 with a bequest from Augustus Ely Silliman of Brooklyn, New York, to bring outstanding scholars in the natural sciences to Yale. A short list of notable presentations over the past century would have to include *The Evolution of*

Modern Medicine by the Canadian physician Sir William Osler, published eight years after it was delivered in 1913. Often referred to today as the "father of modern medicine," Osler had revised most of the text from galley proofs, but with the outbreak of World War I, he immediately became involved in the Allied effort and never completed the alterations. At his death in 1919, the task of finalizing the work was turned over to colleagues. "I propose to take an aëroplane flight through the centuries," he told his audience, "touching only on the tall peaks from which may be had a panoramic view of all the epochs through which we pass."

Another posthumously published lecture that maintains a level of celebrity was prepared by John von Neumann, a gifted mathematician who worked on the Manhattan Project during World War II and did groundbreaking work in quantum physics, functional analysis, set theory, topology, economics, numerical analysis, and hydrodynamics, studied what are now called von Neumann algebras, and was a pioneer in a burgeoning new field known as computer science. He died of bone cancer in 1957 before he was able to deliver his Silliman Lecture, a work that compared the human brain with the workings of "man made automata." Published the following year from his preparatory notes, *The Computer and the Brain* opens simply enough: "I begin by discussing some of the principles underlying the systematics and the practice of computing machines."

In *The Realm of the Nebulae* (1936), Edwin Hubble—

a name that ranks in the history of astronomy with Galileo Galilei, Johannes Kepler, and Sir Isaac Newton—discussed the principal observations that had led him to conclude that the universe is expanding, confirming an equation previously arrived at by Albert Einstein. "With increasing distance, our knowledge fades, and fades rapidly," he wrote with uncommon eloquence. "Eventually, we reach the dim boundary—the utmost limits of our telescopes. There, we measure shadows, and we search among ghostly errors of measurement for landmarks that are scarcely more substantial. The search will continue. Not until the empirical resources are exhausted, need we pass on to the dreamy realms of speculation."

Also of note are the Storrs Lectures, inaugurated in 1889 in honor of William L. Storrs, at one time a Connecticut judge and a professor in the Law School. Among the books to emerge: *The Nature of the Judicial Process* (1921), by future Supreme Court justice Benjamin N. Cardozo, on how judges decide cases, and *An Introduction to the Philosophy of Law* (1922), by one-time Harvard Law School dean Roscoe Pound, a leader in the reform of court administration in the United States. Another affiliation that has spanned decades involves the Yale Child Study Center, established in 1911 as a division of the Yale School of Medicine and known in its earliest years as the Yale Clinic of Child Development. The founder, Dr. Arnold Gesell, is considered by many professionals to have been the driving force in the field of child development in the United States. Among his numerous books was *The Atlas of Infant Behavior: A Systematic Delineation of the Forms and Early Growth of Human Behavior Patterns,* a two-volume work published by the Press in 1934 at a retail cost of twenty-five dollars, a hefty sum to charge for a book during the years of the Great Depression, which may explain in part why only 250 sets were printed. The high price of that landmark effort was made necessary by costs involved in reproducing some 3,200 black-and-white photographs, an extraordinary undertaking for any press at the time. Though little known today, the book was based on twenty-five years of research and was distinctive for the unprecedented use it made of photographs that pictured infants in a "vast array of postural attitudes." What made headlines outside professional circles was the method Dr. Gesell and his associates used to get the pictures. *Time* magazine described the process in a feature article:

> For his prime tool Dr. Gesell chose the cinecamera. Money was forthcoming from the Laura Spelman Rockefeller Memorial in 1926, again in 1930 from the Rockefeller Foundation. Tactful emissaries scoured New Haven for young recruits. Hundreds of thousands of feet of cinema film were exposed. From this immense store the picture sequences for the *Atlas* were carefully selected, each picture made from a single cinema film frame. . . .
>
> [The] arena of investigation was a paneled dome, big as an igloo. Two soundless cinecameras rode on tracks up the sides of the dome to the top. Inside was a specially designed clinical crib with accessories. The crib was in focus whatever the position of the cameras. The dome's

interior was flooded with a soft, diffused light. The dome
was encased in a one-way vision screen so that operators
outside could see inside, but the performing infant could
not see outside.

In 1945, Anna Freud, Heinz Hartmann, and Ernst Kris
established *The Psychoanalytic Study of the Child,* the stated
purpose "to provide an annual discourse for psychoanalysts
who were turning back from the chaos and interruption of a
world at war to the systematic consideration of a developmen-
tal psychoanalytic point of view," according to Dr. Albert J.
Solnit, director of the Yale Child Study Center from 1966 to
1983 and a longtime member of the Publications Committee.
By 2007, the Press had published sixty-two volumes in the
series, twenty of them edited by Solnit, who spent fifty-four
years at Yale in a variety of scholarly and clinical capacities;
he died in 2002 at the age of eighty-two.

An Introduction to Metaphysics by the towering twentieth-
century German philosopher Martin Heidegger has had the
unusual distinction of being translated twice for separate Yale
editions. The first rendering into English was done in 1959 by
Ralph Manheim, the second, in 2000, by Gregory Fried and
Richard Polt. "For Heidegger the whole history of human
thought and existence has been dominated and characterized
by man's understanding of being," Manheim wrote in a note
to his translation, pointing out that the book—based on a
lecture Heidegger delivered at the University of Freiburg in
1935—is an investigation into "the meaning of being and the

history of man's understanding of being." That exploration aside—and it has achieved iconic status in the half-century since its appearance—what continues to identify the work most, perhaps, outside of its philosophical considerations, is the author's eyebrow-raising statement made toward the end of the treatise on the matter of National Socialism, which he supported during the war years as a member of the Nazi Party: "The works that are being peddled about nowadays as the philosophy of National Socialism but have nothing whatever to do with the inner truth and greatness of this movement (namely the encounter between global technology and modern man)—have all been written by men fishing in the troubled waters of 'values' and 'totalities.'"

As a rule, scholarly publishing and best sellers are not concepts that one might normally discuss in the same conversation, but every university press has examples of books that were published for reasons having little to do with enormous revenue potential yet which sold exceedingly well anyway, to the chagrin of marketing directors on the trade side of publishing. "Scholarly books are supposed to serve knowledge, not the marketplace," was one grousing complaint heard in 1978 by the publishing columnist for the *New York Times* Herbert Mitgang, to which Jack Putnam, then executive director of the Association of American University Presses, blithely replied, "University presses are allowed to accumulate profits," especially if their goal is to underwrite the publication of other titles not likely to do well at the cash register. The steady sales of *The Chicago Manual of Style,* first published in 1906 by the University of Chicago Press and by 2008 still going strong in a fifteenth edition, and the continuing popularity of *The Columbia Encyclopedia* through six editions over eight decades by Columbia University Press—including an online version made available in 2007—have set enviable standards for longevity. Not to be overlooked in this context are the Loeb Classical Library at Harvard, an indispensable series of five hundred volumes of Greek and Roman writings from antiquity issued in editions featuring Greek and Latin texts on the verso, or left-hand, pages, with authoritative English translations on the recto, or right, and the Bollingen Press editions at Princeton of the works of such authors as Carl Jung, Samuel Taylor Coleridge, and Paul Valéry, one hundred titles in all, comprising two hundred and fifty volumes, including an edition of *The I Ching or Book of Changes* that by itself has recorded sales of close to a million copies. The University of California Press claims two titles that each surpassed sales of a million copies: *Ishi in Two Worlds: A Biography of the Last Wild Indian of North America* (1961), by Theodora Kroeber, and *The Teachings of Don Juan: A Yaqui Way of Knowledge* (1968), by Carlos Castaneda. At Johns Hopkins University Press, *The 36-Hour Day: A Family Guide to Caring for Persons with Alzheimer Disease, Related Dementing Illnesses, and Memory Loss in Later Life,* by Nancy L. Mace and Peter V. Rabins, observed its silver anniversary in 2006 with release of a fourth edition and reported sales over that period of about a million copies.

One of the most unlikely success stories—and indisputably a work that rates the blockbuster tag—was the publication in 1984 of Tom Clancy's thriller *The Hunt for Red October,* a work of popular fiction that had been rejected by numerous trade publishers before being acquired by the Naval Institute Press, a not-for-profit publisher and member of the Association of American University Presses, and that launched one of the most successful careers in commercial publishing of the twentieth century. Certainly one of the most satisfying publishing stories of the past several decades was the posthumous publication of John Kennedy Toole's *Confederacy of Dunces,* a work of experimental fiction uniformly rejected throughout the trade as too avant-garde but published by Louisiana State University Press in 1980 at the urging of the novelist Walker Percy. The novel went on to win the Pulitzer Prize and the National Book Award, scoring admirable sales in the process. The University of Texas Press, meanwhile, had a best seller in 1977 with *The Book of Merlyn* by T. H. White, the fifth book of the Arthurian epic; *One Writer's Beginnings,* a charming memoir of growing up in Mississippi by the great Southern writer Eudora Welty, made its way onto the New York Times Best-Seller List shortly after its release in 1984 by Harvard University Press. A true oddity among scholarly imprints was the publication in 1974 by the University of Alabama Press of *Storyville, New Orleans: Being an Authentic, Illustrated Account of the Notorious Red-Light District,* by Al Rose, not so much for the saucy nature of the subject matter, but for the fact that the work became the basis of Louis Malle's 1978 film, *Pretty Baby*, starring Brooke Shields, David Carradine, and Susan Sarandon. Though rare, this example of a university press title making it big in Hollywood is not unique; in 1992, Robert Redford directed an adaptation of Norman Maclean's best-selling autobiographical novella, *A River Runs through It*. Published in 1976 by the University of Chicago Press, the film version featured Brad Pitt, Craig Sheffer, and Tom Skerritt in the leading roles and won an Academy Award for cinematography.

At Yale University Press, the remarkable sales of two titles issued within six years of each other in the 1950s are interesting for reasons that go well beyond the number of copies each sold, though in both instances the figures they recorded—and which they continue to post after more than half a century in print—are wildly successful by any measurement of accounting. The first of these is the kind of book that a university press exists to publish. Brilliantly titled, in what had to be a moment of inspiration, *The Lonely Crowd*, the book grew out of research conducted in 1948 and 1949 by David Riesman at the invitation of the Yale Committee on National Policy. A respected sociologist and one-time constitutional lawyer who clerked for Justice Louis Brandeis, Riesman was assisted by two colleagues, Reuel Denney and Nathan Glazer. "Our study was an ambitious effort at synthesis," he explained several years later, describing their work in New Haven as a telling example of what in recent times has been called an "interdisciplinary approach" to scholarship, which in this case involved examination of materials in philosophy, history, popular culture, psychoanalysis, and sociology.

Among its many claims to fame, *The Lonely Crowd* introduced such terms as "inner-directed" and "other-directed" that have since become idiomatic expressions in the language, and was a pioneer in describing what it called a "self-conscious society." Issued in a modest first printing of fifteen hundred copies in 1950, the book began to attract a general audience. One of the first hints that it would reach a readership that went well beyond the immediate circle of professional sociologists came in an essay by the noted literary critic Lionel Trilling for the *Griffin*, a book club journal, which went so far as to suggest that social science might replace fiction as a vehicle for understanding society. "It sort of staggered everyone, it kept selling and kept selling, and about the time it had sold four or five hundred thousand copies, it was licensed to Anchor Books as a trade paperback," John Ryden told me. "When Yale got the rights back, it sold another seven or eight hundred thousand copies." With close to one and a half million copies sold to date, *The Lonely Crowd* is a prime example of what an academic press does best. It began its existence as a research project conducted at the behest of a major university, and the findings were reported to the world by a publishing entity that carried the name of the sponsoring institution. Just as relevant, it stimulated a dialogue—people outside the academy talked about it with earnestness and conviction—and was controversial in productive ways.

According to a 1997 study conducted by the sociologist Herbert J. Gans, *The Lonely Crowd* is the best-selling book in the history of American sociology. In a foreword to the 2001 Yale Nota Bene paperback edition, Todd Gitlin, a professor of culture, journalism, and sociology at New York University, speculated on the factors that made all this happen. "With unerring hindsight we can see that it sympathetically exposed the anxieties of a middle class that was rising with the postwar boom, suburbanizing, busy availing itself of upgraded homes, machines, and status, relieved to be done with the Depression and the war but baffled by cultural and psychological upheavals beneath the surface of everyday life." Just as significant, Gitlin wrote, the book was "jargon-free" and "lucidly written, with a knack for puckish phrases." Although "demanding of the serious reader, and scarcely written in sound bites, it had the sound of an agreeable human voice, by turns chatty and approachably awkward, graceful and warm, nuanced and colloquial, sober and avuncular, but frequently casual and good humored. Unlike most academic treatises, it did not get bogged down in definitional chatter." The book accomplished everything, in short, that a serious work of scholarly inquiry is supposed to do and turned a tidy profit for one and all in the process.

Just six years after that remarkable achievement came a triumph of another kind entirely. The publication of fiction is not generally perceived as being within the province of scholarly publishing, though some presses—Louisiana State University, Nebraska, and Northwestern among them—do include new works of contemporary writers on their lists, while new editions of classic works are staples on most others. The Oxford and Cambridge editions of the works of Shakespeare and Milton, the ongoing program of the University of California Press to publish the entire oeuvre of Samuel Langhorne Clemens, its handsome editions of Dante and Virgil with original woodcuts by the artist Barry Moser, the University of Oklahoma Press variorum editions of Geoffrey Chaucer come immediately to mind, and there are so many more, but works of the imagination, for the most part, are issued by trade publishers.

There was nothing at all typical about the playwright Eugene O'Neill and the publication by Yale University Press in 1956 of *Long Day's Journey into Night*. At the time of his death in 1953 at the age of sixty-four, O'Neill's renown was firmly established; he was presented with a Nobel Prize for Literature in 1936, and three of his plays—*Beyond the Horizon* (1920), *Anna Christie* (1922), and *Strange Interlude* (1928)—received Pulitzer Prizes. His vast body of work, meanwhile, had found an agreeable home with Bennett Cerf at the firm of Boni and Liveright, and then at Random House, which Cerf cofounded in 1927 with Donald Klopfer. In *At Random*, a totally engaging volume of publishing reminiscences, Cerf declared O'Neill to be "the most beautiful man I ever met, and when I say beautiful, I mean in the sense that to look at him was soul-satisfying," and when Cerf gave his word that he would not publish the play for at least twenty-five years after the playwright's death, he kept it. O'Neill had decided to keep the searingly autobiographical play under lock and key for a variety of personal reasons, not least among them the revealing examination he included of his mother's drug addiction. Eight years before he died, O'Neill turned the completed manuscript over to Cerf in a manner that took on the aura of a formal ceremony. "When O'Neill gave us the script of *Long Day's Journey,* he wanted to seal it up," Cerf told Arthur and Barbara Gelb, the playwright's biographers. "He insisted it be done with red sealing wax. We sent out for some, but when it arrived, none of us knew how to use it. We used up two boxes of matches and got wax all over our hands before we finally managed to seal the envelope that held the script." Before leaving, O'Neill dictated and signed a statement that expressed his wishes, then asked Cerf to countersign the document and deposit it in the Random House vault along with the manuscript.

According to a number of accounts, O'Neill had been anxious to protect his son, Eugene O'Neill, Jr., a teacher in the Classics Department at Yale, from suffering any undue embarrassment that might emerge from the family disclosures, but that concern became moot with the son's untimely death in 1950, though no formal revocation was ever made. Hard on the heels of her husband's death three years later, Carlotta Monterey O'Neill—sole legatee, executrix, and owner of all rights to her husband's work—took steps to publish the play and mount a theatrical production. "We put the manuscript in our safe, fully intending to abide by his wishes; but soon after he died we learned that Carlotta had a different view: she demanded that we ignore Gene's directive and proceed with publishing the play at once," Cerf wrote. "We refused, of course, but then were horrified to learn that legally all the cards were in her hand; what the author wanted, and what he had asked us to do, had no validity if *she* wanted something else—which she did. When we insisted that Random House could not in conscience publish it, she demanded that we give her the manuscript—it was her legal property—and Yale University Press, apparently caring as little as she did about what O'Neill had wanted, published it promptly. They therefore had a best seller on their hands and a Book-of-the-Month Club selection, but I do not regret that we took the stand we did, because I still think we were right." Sensitive to charges that Yale had perhaps jumped too enthusiastically at publishing what was clearly a seductive target of opportunity, University Librarian James T. Babb wrote a letter to the *New York Times* asserting that publication of the manuscript—which had become the university's property—proceeded only after the library had "been assured" by Carlotta O'Neill "that the playwright had lifted his original restriction."

Cerf did not come right out and say in his memoir that a principal reason he may have rebuffed Carlotta was because he disliked her intensely, but his antipathy for her is nowhere disguised in his memoir. "Carlotta didn't want him to have a good time; she wanted to own him," he wrote about the way she seemed to bully O'Neill around in public. "As time went on, Carlotta became more and more irrational," he declared elsewhere, suggesting in no uncertain terms that she was close to being certifiably insane. And there was this little tidbit: "When Gene would go into one of his Irish furies, he would hurl things at Carlotta. He once threw a wall mirror at her, and if it had hit her, it might have killed her."

Yale, in any case, was a perfect choice for Carlotta to turn by virtue of a long-standing relationship her husband had enjoyed with the university. In 1926, Yale had presented the playwright with an honorary degree, the only time he accepted such an honor, which he did in this instance as a gesture of friendship to George Pierce Baker, head of the university's Drama Department and his workshop professor at Harvard in 1914 and 1915. O'Neill's son, moreover, earned his bachelor and doctoral degrees from Yale, and the university's Sterling Library had been designated the repository of his literary archives.

Publication of the play in 1956 was timed to coincide with a premier production in Stockholm. A successful run there led to a standing-room-only opening on Broadway, with Fredric March, Florence Eldridge, Jason Robards, and Bradford Dillman in the starring roles. Tony awards for 1957 followed for best play and best actor for March; an unprecedented fourth Pulitzer Prize for O'Neill ensued. Sales, meanwhile, proceeded at a giddy pace. A first printing of five thousand copies sold out within three days, qualifying *Long Day's Journey into Night* as the most briskly selling title in Press history. By the time a fifth printing came along later that year, a corrected line of text was introduced by way of a curious circumstance. Fredric March, a consummate professional with a legendary reputation for wanting to know everything he possibly could about the character he was playing—in this instance James Tyrone, the male lead—had been puzzled by the meaning and context of a line in the play he was required to say: "God bless you, K.O."

When the production came to the Shubert in New Haven for a pre-Broadway tune-up, March had an opportunity to ask Donald Gallup, curator of the Collection of American Literature at Yale's Beinecke Library, if he had any idea what O'Neill had meant. Gallup chose to go directly to the source—the playwright's holographic manuscript, and not the typescript copied from the original by Carlotta, which had been used for the play. His discovery of a dropped line proved exceedingly significant. Here is what O'Neill had written, and what his wife had missed: "God bless you, Kid. (*His eyes close. He mumbles.*) That last drink—the old K.O." The very evening of that discovery, March delivered the recovered line on stage, and it has remained in every production since. By the time the sixty-first printing came around in 1989, another major correction had been discovered by textual scholars, this one clarifying the drug addiction of O'Neill's mother with the restoration of these lines: "It's a special kind of medicine. I have to take it because there is no other that can stop the pain—all the pain—I mean in my hands." For the play's golden anniversary as a Yale title, a new paperback edition featuring bright new cover art was issued. Total sales at that time were reported at one and a half million copies, with sales today averaging ten thousand a year, a good many of them to students of American literature who are required to read the play in their classes. The Press also publishes five other O'Neill titles: *Touch of the Poet, Moon for the Misbegotten, A Touch of the Poet and More Stately Mansions, The Iceman Cometh,* and *Collected Shorter Plays.*

For all of these impressive achievements—and they truly were noteworthy—George Parmly Day was an amateur publisher whose primary duty at Yale was to oversee the university's finances, not manage the day-to-day operations of an academic press, and certainly not to formulate a scrupulously balanced publishing list year in and year out. At his death in 1959, the *New York Times* obituary called him the "greatest fund raiser in Yale's history" and credited him with having increased the institution's endowment during his tenure as treasurer from $12 million to $101 million, a paltry figure by today's standards—the endowment in 2007 was $22.5 billion —but quite impressive for its time all the same.

Over at the Press, where he wore his second hat, Day maintained a corps of trusted lieutenants in key senior positions, each a loyal Yale graduate, each a member of a tightly knit community that answered directly to him. The stunning variety of important titles they ushered through the Press during their watch, and the high literary standards they took care to maintain, speak eloquently enough for themselves,

especially during a period when faculty representation on the
Publications Committee was minimal. Indeed, on a few occasions books were published for reasons having more to do with
the personal and political views of the men who guided the
Press—which until 1961 remained an independently owned
entity operated apart from Yale—and less to do with scholarship, a situation that led to growing oversight from the
administration and ultimately to a revamped Publications
Committee that would have a significant say in how the Press
goes about its business.

This delicate circumstance was implied, however cur-
sorily, by Chester Kerr, Yale Class of 1936, secretary of the
Governing Board from 1949 to 1959 and director from 1959 to
1979, in an informal reminiscence he wrote for a 1983 pamphlet
to mark the seventy-fifth anniversary of the Press's founding.
"When some of his activities became somewhat debatable
during the exigencies of World War II," Kerr wrote of Day, "it
fell to President Charles Seymour, '08, to suggest to Mr. Day
that perhaps he should surrender the executive role of director
and content himself with the chairmanship of the board. To
emphasize that the University had assumed a greater degree
of control over its publishing arm, President Seymour asked
Edgar S. Furniss, already Provost of the University and Dean
of the Graduate School, to add the title of Director of the
Press to his portfolio."

Kerr offered no insight as to just what those "somewhat
debatable" activities may have been during that period, and

little light is shed in the minutes of the Publications Commit-tee or the Governing Board. But there are hints, at least, as to how publishing priorities were modified after December 7, 1941, and how they would continue during the war and the immediate aftermath. On January 19, 1942, just six weeks after the attack on Pearl Harbor occasioned the onset of hostilities with Japan and Germany, the Governing Board discussed at length what role it should take in support of the American cause. According to the minutes, "It was agreed that from now on we must consider more carefully than ever before the character and quality of all manuscripts submitted for publication, and redouble our efforts to make sure that every volume issued under the imprint of the Press is of undoubted service and of real value in its field. With this end in view it was recognized that it may well prove necessary for the Press to defer indefinitely the publication of certain books which cannot fairly be described as being of immediate importance, desirable as reasonably prompt publication of them might have been considered in normal times."

The board members also agreed that the Press "should in general continue its policy of publishing books which through their literary, analytical or other values help in clarifying the national and international problems now confronting us," and cited three volumes published the previous year as ex-amples of "a good contribution from the Press to the welfare of our country." They included *The Armed Forces of the Pacific*, a military assessment of Japanese naval strength by American navy captain W. D. Puleston; *Good Neighbors: Argentina, Brazil, Chile and Seventeen Other Countries,* by Hubert Herring, a respected historian of Latin American affairs and politics; and *Where Stands a Winged Sentry,* an inspirational account of surviving the Nazi bombardment of England during the Battle of Britain by the novelist Margaret Kennedy, written in the form of a journal and published within months of the air assault. Publishing in general declined in the weeks following Pearl Harbor, and Yale was no exception. Twenty-one university presses were operating in the United States at the time, with Columbia, by far, being the most active, issuing 92 of the 551 scholarly titles released in 1941; Yale finished a distant fifth that year, behind Harvard, Princeton, and the University of Chicago.

The minutes of the April 27, 1942, meeting of the Governing Board included an entry that speaks for the period and pointedly demonstrates the sometimes esoteric nature of books published by a university press and the limited audience so many of them are able to reach: "Mr. Day reported that the Secretary had written to about two hundred authors, whose books had sold less than five copies during the past year, offering to give the authors a limited number of complimentary copies of their books if they would permit the Press to dispose of surplus sheets of waste paper and to sell the plates as an aid to national defense, and also release the Press from making any further reports or accountings on the titles involved." It was further reported that 130 authors had readily agreed to the offer and that the Press "had already been able to release nearly seven tons of metal for which we have been paid about $900."

The decision to part company with one author in particular, though, was probably made for reasons having little to do with surplus paper or cumbersome metal type. In 1941, a move was made to sever ties with the expatriate poet, critic, and translator Ezra Pound, who had published two books with the Press a decade earlier. With a minimum of ceremony, the rights to *ABC of Reading*—a concise literary primer issued in 1934 that has lost none of its intellectual bite by the passage of seven decades—were reverted to the author, and the book was declared out of print. Copies of *Make It New*, a volume of critical essays from the previous twenty years published in 1935, remained available through the 1940s while Pound was living in Italy, but with just a smattering of volumes sold. In a letter dated March 25, 1949, the Press advised Pound's wife, Dorothy, that $26.32 in royalties had been earned through that whole period. Four years earlier, Pound had been brought back to the United States to face charges of treason stemming from his pro-Fascist activities during the war that included the airing of three hundred anti-American and anti-Semitic broadcasts. Declared mentally incompetent to stand trial, he was confined to Saint Elizabeths Hospital in Washington, D.C., before being released in 1958 and allowed to return to Italy, where he died in 1972 at the age of eighty-seven.

By war's end, all of Pound's American publishers but one —New Directions—had discontinued publishing his books.

Bennett Cerf, cofounder of Random House and publisher of the Modern Library, went a step further and ordered the removal of a dozen Pound poems from an anthology of American and English poetry to be released in 1946, a move that set off a storm of protest among many prominent writers who felt that art should be kept separate from politics. Cerf soon agreed to restore the poems in a later edition, proclaiming himself an "angry convert" to the arguments that had been posed, stating he was doing so "in order to remove any possible hint of suppression, and because we concede that it may be wrong to confuse Pound the poet and Pound the man." Cerf also made clear that the new volume would contain these defiant words: "Here he is. Pound the man we consider a contemptible betrayer of his country." But a strong reaction from Julien Cornell, Pound's lawyer, threatening a libel action—the poet had never been convicted of treason in a court of law, after all—persuaded Cerf to modify his comments and delete these two sentences.

Meanwhile, James Laughlin, the founder and owner of New Directions, seized the opportunity to acquire publishing rights to all of Pound's works. Laughlin had always credited a meeting with Pound in Italy in 1936 with inspiring him to become a publisher at the age of twenty-two and was eager to promote the man's work, which he did starting in 1938 with *Guide to Kulchur*. Two years later, Laughlin picked up the *Cantos* from Farrar and Rinehart. "From that point on, we did one Pound book a year," he told Linda Kuehl in a lengthy profile published in the *New York Times* in 1973. Asked directly how he felt about "the criticism leveled against you at the time for publishing" Pound, Laughlin said, "It never bothered me because I knew the man was a genius. We all have our aberrations." The first New Directions edition of *ABC of Reading* was issued in 1951 as part of its New Classics Series and by 2007 had gone through no fewer than thirty printings in cloth and paperback. (In a 1983 interview with *Paris Review*, Laughlin named *ABC of Reading* one of the three best-selling Pound titles on his backlist.) Reviewing the 1951 reissue in the *New York Times*, Harvey Breit wrote that "an admiration for Ezra Pound must begin and end with literature: the political Pound is monstrous. But the literary Pound is lovely." Many of the essays included in *Make It New* were incorporated in a volume of Pound's work titled *Literary Essays*, published jointly in 1954 by New Directions in the United States and Faber and Faber in England; it also remains in print.

When George Parmly Day stepped down as director of the Press in 1944 to become chairman of the board, he was replaced by Edgar S. Furniss, with operational responsibility entrusted to Norman V. Donaldson, Class of 1915. Donaldson had come to work for Day in the marketing department four years after receiving his bachelor's degree and a year after a tour in the navy during World War I as skipper of a submarine chaser that earned him a Navy Cross; he was named managing director. "I've always been on the managerial side, not the editorial side," Donaldson told the Yale University News

Bureau when he retired in 1959 after forty years with the Press: "Maybe you'd call me the housekeeper." For editorial decisions, Furniss and Donaldson would rely on Eugene Davidson, Yale '26, who had joined the Press as an editor in 1931 and now was named editor of the Press as part of the new management team, though not without a murmur of discord, according to Chester Kerr, who maintained that Davidson's appointment came to the "consternation of a growing number of Yale faculty" because of an apparent propensity "to inflict his personal political views on the output" of the publishing list. Among Davidson's perceived transgressions were his ready willingness to acquire the works of certain "scholars"—and Kerr put *scholars* in quotation marks—who were, in his words, "partial to the isolationist, anti-FDR, anti-USSR, pro-German stances of the day." Kerr alleged that there were a "host" of these authors on Davidson's lists but cited just three by name: Ludwig von Mises, David J. Dallin, and Charles A. Beard, each a highly controversial figure of the mid-twentieth century whose writings occasioned heated reactions from economists, historians, other academics, and reviewers throughout the country. Kerr did not elaborate on his volatile charges, however, and left his teasing commentary at that, though a close examination of the titles he undoubtedly had in mind, and the sometimes hostile reactions they engendered, is instructive, since the operating structure of the Press and the course it would pursue from that point on to now were sharpened as a result.

Between 1942 and 1955, Yale University Press published

thirteen books written by von Mises, Dallin, and Beard that put forth unambiguous points of view during a time of global strife and Cold War. Kerr's denigration of their fitness notwithstanding, the central issue is not so much whether the three had the credentials to write for a distinguished academic press— Beard and von Mises in particular had impressive résumés featuring books published with respected trade houses—but whether their manuscripts were approved because their ideas happened to agree with the political beliefs of the editor in charge and promoted causes that he embraced.

Eugene Davidson, it bears pointing out, was by no means coy about his views. A prolific writer and poet, he wrote regularly for the *Saturday Review,* the *New Yorker,* the *Yale Review,* and the *Progressive.* A talented linguist who included Chinese among his languages, Davidson was director of the Foundation for Foreign Affairs from 1957 to 1970 and for many years chaired an international symposium called the Conference on European Problems, becoming the group's honorary president in 1986. After leaving Yale in 1959, he became editor of *Modern Age,* a quarterly based in Chicago to which he also contributed commentary throughout his ten-year tenure there; a collection of his pieces for the journal, *Reflections on a Disruptive Decade: Essays on the Sixties,* was published by the University of Missouri Press in 2000. Davidson's other books—all written after he left Yale and described generally by reviewers as revisionist works of mid-twentieth-century history—included *The Nuremberg Fallacy, The Making of Adolf*

Hitler, and *The Unmaking of Adolf Hitler;* he died in 2002 at the age of ninety-nine.

David J. Dallin, on the other hand, was neither an academic nor a professional writer before he wrote his first book for Yale. A Russian revolutionary leader who belonged to the moderate Menshevik faction that split from the Bolsheviks in 1903, Dallin fled to Germany in 1921, a year before V. I. Lenin banned the movement. With the rise of Hitler, Dallin, a Jew, was forced into exile a second time, and moved to the United States in 1940, where he promptly began writing books and articles about his homeland and its leaders, acquiring a reputation as a strident anti-Communist and commentator on Soviet politics. His first book, *Soviet Russia's Foreign Policy, 1939–1942,* was issued two years after his arrival in America and was followed in quick succession by *Russia and Postwar Europe* (1943), *The Real Soviet Russia* (1944), *The Big Three: The United States, Britain, Russia* (1945), *Forced Labor in Soviet Russia* (1947, with Boris I. Nicolaevsky), *Soviet Russia and the Far East* (1948), *The Rise of Russia in Asia* (1949), and *The New Soviet Empire* (1951). Dallin's robust productivity was such that it merited commendation at a meeting of the Executive Committee of the Governing Board on January 10, 1955, where Donaldson noted that combined sales of the titles had totaled sixty thousand volumes, tidy numbers for an academic press that often measured success in the hundreds. Better yet, Donaldson enthused, more was on the way; *Soviet Espionage* and *The Changing World of Soviet Russia* would appear in print in 1955 and 1956, respectively. Dallin's next book after those, *Soviet Foreign Policy after Stalin,* did not bear the Yale imprint, rather that of J. P. Lippincott of Philadelphia, a trade house—and it appeared in 1961, two years after Davidson left New Haven for Chicago.

The general reception to Dallin's work in academic circles was summed up at an international symposium in 2006 by two historians of Soviet Russia, John Earl Haynes of the Library of Congress and his frequent collaborator, Harvey Klehr. "David Dallin's *Soviet Espionage* provided a thorough and judicious summary of what was known in 1955," they noted. "Not himself an academic, Dallin's personal interest in Soviet espionage drew him to gather much of what was publicly available into a Yale University Press book. But in the latter half of the 1960s an increasingly hostile academic community dismissed Dallin's book on the grounds that most of his evidence consisted of the testimony of defectors and exiles and the results of congressional and FBI investigations. Such evidence was increasingly distrusted, and Dallin's Menshevik past was taken as reason for skepticism as well."

For his part, Davidson was unfazed by the assault that had been mounted against his prize author, and he declared as much in the first essay he wrote for *Modern Age,* a journal, in his words, that was committed to "search out the roots and forms of conservatism." The 1960 piece, titled "Mr. Dallin among the Scholars," did not mention Yale University Press by name but did cite four of the titles Dallin wrote that were issued under its imprint and credited them with telling "some new things" to American readers. "These extraordinary insights accumulated in Dallin's books as he clearly saw the direction and purpose of Soviet politics that were so baffling to so many in high places." Among those who purportedly were baffled—and it was the central thrust of Davidson's brief essay—were the "tried and true reviewers among the academic critics," a circumstance he found especially irksome. "Despite the evidence with which he supported his analyses," he wrote of Dallin, "the reception of his books in academic circles was always less than enthusiastic. Although he had scattered admirers among the professoriat he had far more opponents, who ranged from the violently hostile to those who merely called him anti-Soviet and who said in effect that even if he was right he made the future look too grim, that we must try to see a better face on our Russian allies or they would never have one."

Writing specifically about Dallin's 1947 book for Yale, *Forced Labor in Soviet Russia*, Davidson made this claim: "It is not too much to say that thousands of people owe their freedom to the events set in motion by this book. But it had made its way against the academic procession," the same academic procession, presumably, that Davidson had worked with so closely over three decades as a senior editor at a major academic press. "What are the causes of this *trahison des clercs?*" he asked, using a French phrase popularized in the 1920s by the French writer Julien Benda that translates as "treason of the intellectuals," which prompted him to follow with yet another question: "Why did these scholarly books arouse the wrath or passive resistance of scholars?" Though the answer was not forthcoming, Davidson promised to explore the matter in the years to come. "For reasons which we shall pursue in future issues of *Modern Age,* too many intellectuals have consciously or unconsciously placed their hopes for the good society in a totalitarian system that has betrayed these docile admirers over and over again."

Ludwig von Mises was an Austrian economist of Jewish ancestry who, like Dallin, fled the Nazis and took up residence in the United States; a prominent educator in his native land, he became known for free-market views that were so rigid that a center of political theory espousing them was established in his name in Alabama in 1981 by Llewellyn H. Rockwell, Jr., a frequent contributor to the *Wall Street Journal* and the *Washington Times.* Espousing views said to have had a profound effect on the policies of Ronald Reagan, von Mises championed the libertarian doctrine that regards with intense suspicion any government intervention in the economy. He produced three books under Davidson's auspices, *Bureaucracy* and *Omnipotent Government: The Rise of the Total State and Total War* (both 1944) and a reworked English version of his 1940 work, *Nationalökonomie,* published in 1949 by Yale under the title *Human Action: A Treatise on Economics* and regarded today as an essential manifesto for what is known as the Austrian School of Economics. The reviews of *Human Action* followed predictable lines—readers on the far right were dazzled, those in the middle and on the left utterly dismayed—though one piece written for the *New York Times* by the Harvard economist John Kenneth Galbraith took dead aim at Yale University Press itself, not the author. Printed under the headline "In Defense of Laissez-Faire," Galbraith devoted nearly a third of his commentary to the laudatory description of the book printed on the dust jacket:

> I come now to the publisher. However much one may disagree with Professor Mises, he is a learned man and a famous teacher. The market, in spite of its virtues, does not pay for all the books that deserve publication and it is therefore both appropriate and good that a university press made this one available. But surely it should do so with some obligation to scholarly restraint.
>
> The publisher's statement on the jacket of the book says that Professor Mises' approach bears little relation to what is "usually taught in classrooms or to the hopeful, revolutionary but bankrupt 'economics' that conquered the Western World in the last decades." It adverts to the "malignant" political consequences of actions during the last decade at variance with Professor Mises' views.
>
> Does the Yale University Press stand on this comprehensive slur on present-day economics, including that taught in the classrooms at New Haven? What are the "malignant" consequences of not having followed Professor Mises' advice in the last decade?
>
> Does the publisher believe with him, for example, that the war should have been fought without any

allocation, priority, price or other controls apart from high taxes and inflation? Those controls were disagreeable—possibly one had to administer them to know how really disagreeable they were—but what of the alternatives and their risk? Surely someone associated with this publishing venture, if only in what seemed like innocent emulation, got sadly out of bounds.

In a tightly edited letter to the editor published in the *New York Times*—there are five sets of ellipses in the printed version—Davidson argued that the dust jacket endorsement "merely attempts to condense" von Mises's views. "It is an important thesis of the book, and therefore of the jacket copy," he argued, "that government intervention in the market economy produced systems of increasing economic and political coercion that have led to totalitarianism in some countries and to near bankruptcy in others." The economic texts used in Yale classrooms, he continued, "are certainly very different from Professor von Mises' book, which is an attempt to establish a scientific and philosophical basis for the whole problem of human thought." Responding to Galbraith's sharpest question, Davidson offered the following: "The war, the forced migrations of peoples, inflation and scarcity, the decreasing areas of individual freedom even in the West, these are the malignant consequences, Professor von Mises believes, of wrong economic decisions—to name a few."

An even stronger reaction greeted publication of two monographs by Charles A. Beard, a former professor of history at Columbia University who helped found the New School for Social Research in New York. In the years leading up to World War II, Beard was a vocal advocate of isolationism and a strong opponent of American participation in the conflict. No stranger to controversy, he had resigned his Columbia professorship in 1917 to protest the university's expulsion of two colleagues who had opposed U.S. participation in World War I. "I have been driven to the conclusion that the university is really under the control of a small and active group of trustees who are reactionary and visionless in politics and narrow and medieval in religion," he wrote in his letter of resignation to Nicholas Murray Butler, Columbia's president.

His publishing credits included more than thirty works of history issued over three decades by numerous trade publishing houses, though his increasingly revisionist views during a time of profound international uncertainty left him with no commercial publisher for *American Foreign Policy in the Making, 1932–1940: A Study in Responsibilities* (1946) and *President Roosevelt and the Coming of the War, 1941: A Study in Appearances and Realities* (1948), his final two efforts, which found a home at Yale. Among the themes put forth repeatedly in those books was the angry accusation that President Roosevelt had attempted secretly to bring the United States into war. "I think the Charles Beard episode, in my opinion, is the one time that Yale Press really stepped out of bounds, if bounds are defined by keeping yourself focused on scholarship and not getting involved directly in politics," the Yale historian Gaddis Smith told me. "I mean you can publish scholarly books that certainly have a political objective," but these books, he stressed, were "nothing more than bitter polemical attacks on FDR."

Just six months before his death on September 1, 1948, Beard, a former president of the American Historical Association, was presented with a gold medal from the National Institute of Arts and Letters, an award given once every ten years. "Lewis Mumford, the writer, resigned in a protest against Dr. Beard's isolationist stand before and during the war," the *New York Times* reported in Beard's obituary. "Other members of the institute, however, explained that the award was given for 'a whole life's work.'"

Given the dearth of anecdotal material to survive from that period, one can only speculate on the impact this growing unease for the work of these three highly visible authors had on the Yale faculty, particularly those in the Economics Department. But a few hints suggest that everything was not business as usual and that pressure was being brought to bear, however gently it may appear today in the notes kept of Press discussions. At a meeting of the Executive Committee on May 10, 1948, the chief topic was whether all future books bearing the Yale imprint should include a statement of clarification asserting that "publications on controversial issues" must not be regarded "as designed to reflect the views of the officers of the University or the collective opinions of the faculty since the Yale imprint appears on important writings of every variety of opinion." The three members present that day, Edgar Furniss, Eugene Davidson, and Norman Donaldson (George Parmly Day was absent), voted to submit the statement—they did not call it a "disclaimer"—to the Governing Board the following week for approval, where it met with resistance from some members not identified in the minutes, but presumably faculty members, since none of them were at the meeting a week earlier, where the proposal sailed through without any apparent opposition at all. After what appears to have been a lengthy discussion, President Seymour, who also attended the meeting, suggested that the matter be referred "for advice" to the University Council's Committee on Publications. The proposal must have been scuttled at that level, because it does not appear again in any Press minutes, and disclaimers never became a fixture in Yale books.

Yet another episode of faculty opposition to Press policy made its way into the minutes of the Executive Committee meetings and involved a series of books already cleared for publication. Chester Kerr devoted a single sentence to the imbroglio in his 1983 reminiscence, but what he had to relate in that brief mention spoke volumes: "Perhaps the loudest outcry arose when, in deference to corporate outrage over the publication of too 'liberal' a view of the oil industry by a young Law School professor named Eugene V. Rostow, Yale 1932, the Press contracted to publish three studies in reply—all subsidized by the American Petroleum Institute."

The book in question by Rostow, *A National Policy for the Oil Industry*, was published in 1948 and "unfavorably received by most members" of the oil industry, according to a scholarly essay in the *Journal of Political Economy*, the charge being that the book made "sweeping recommendations" that were "based on inaccurate information and analysis." No author can satisfy every reader all the time, but the American Petroleum Institute took its displeasure in this case a step further by presenting Yale University Press with a grant that would "enable well-qualified scholars to make a free inquiry in the industry without censorship" and to "ascertain the facts that bear on the industry's problems of production and distribution, questions of prices and markets and allied problems." The result was the formation by the Press of what was called the Petroleum Monograph Series and the publication of three books: *Price Making and Price Behavior in the Petroleum Industry* (volume 1, 1954), by Ralph Cassady, Jr.; *Conservation in the Production of Petroleum: A Study in Industrial Control* (volume 2, 1957), by Erich Zimmermann; and *Integration and Competition in the Petroleum Industry* (volume 3, 1959), by Melvin G. de Chazeau and Alfred E. Kahn.

A four-page preface to the Petroleum Monograph Series went to exceptional lengths to state in forceful terms how the authors researching and writing the three books were named by an independent board of "four professional economists not connected with the petroleum industry and two experienced oilmen." The source of the funding was disclosed, along with assurances that no restrictions whatsoever were placed on the "degree of academic freedom" that had been granted to the authors. Still, the lobbyists must have been pleased with the results. Beyond funding the project—which included "honoraria, travel, and other outlays incurred by the authors, an Editorial Board, and the Press"—they also bought many copies of the finished books and made sure they were distributed far and wide. The copy of volume 1 in the series I perused, borrowed from the Dinand Library of the College of the Holy Cross in Worcester, Massachusetts, has a bookplate that identifies it as a "Gift of the American Petroleum Institute."

Despite the Press's effort to disclose the arrangement, the faculty was not pleased with the precedent that had been set. When all was said and done, the fact remained that three commissioned rebuttals to a monograph written by a distinguished member of the Yale faculty had been financed by the very industry he had profiled and had been published by the same academic press. While this was going on, Chester Kerr had been hired by the Press and appointed secretary of the board, and he was keeping notes of committee meetings. Indeed, Kerr maintained that the title secretary of the Board of Governors itself had been invented especially for him at the urging of President A. Whitney Griswold in order to place him "squarely between Messrs. Donaldson and Davidson." Kerr's unease with Davidson is apparent from the care he took in reporting the details of sensitive discussions, particularly those he claimed a quarter-century later he strongly disagreed with. A meeting of the Committee on Publications on January 14, 1952, for instance, is revealing. The prospect of the Press contracting for a third book with von Mises, and concerns surrounding the petroleum series, were among the items on the docket. Lloyd Reynolds, chairman of the Department of Economics, was invited to attend and address the committee. His remarks, though paraphrased by Kerr, were carefully noted. What follows is part of what he had to say about both matters:

> Mr. Reynolds began by saying that he personally had no real concern over the reissuance by the Press of *The Theory of Money and Credit* but that he would like to relate the question to the Press's whole program of publishing in the field of economics. He assured the Committee that the Department of Economics has no wish to influence the Press unduly but added that inevitably what the Press does in this field affects the Department in its public relations. For example, he said, he believed that members of the Department had found themselves in an awkward position in recent years because of the Press's apparent emphasis on books by von Mises and because of the proposed oil industry series.... Mr. Reynolds then pursued the subject of the oil industry series with the observation that in his opinion many members of his profession viewed the project with doubt, that they could not escape the conclusion that when the industry supplied the money for such research, the research might not be entirely objective. He added that he did not think

that the authors selected were the top specialists in their field.

Clearly, things were out of joint here, but it was not until 1959, when Davidson stepped down from the editorship and left for Chicago, that tensions began to ease. There were other key changes—Norman Donaldson was appointed director of the Press at the same time that President Griswold had "encouraged," to quote Chester Kerr, "the establishment of a full-blown faculty Committee on Publications without whose consent no Director or editor could apply the imprint of the Yale University Press." A former professor in the Yale History Department, Griswold had been keen to bring the Press "more into the orbit" of the university, according to John Ryden, Kerr's successor as director of the Press, and it was Griswold who pushed to make it a formal department in 1961. The *Articles of Government* established for the Press makes that point unequivocally in its opening statement, giving Griswold credit for having initiated the policy that led to the move, and for insisting that the Press "cultivate the resources" of the university "and of American scholarship in general," while authorizing the university to assume "the same responsibility toward the Press that it bears in relation to other agencies of scholarship." This was a watershed moment, in other words, and the Press has moved forward ever since, making the graceful transition from an operation that was very good to one that is outstanding.

Kerr named twenty-two faculty members of prominence who served on the Publications Committee in the years that followed, beginning with Frederick Whiley Hilles, Class of 1922, an English literature scholar under whose thirteen-year term (1950–1963) as chairman some 852 new titles had been approved for publication. Kerr singled out the contributions of Leonard W. Doob, Ralph S. Brown, Jr., Jaroslav Pelikan, G. Evelyn Hutchinson, Robert A. Dahl, C. Vann Woodward, Louis L. Martz, Dr. Albert J. Solnit, John E. Smith, David Potter, Dr. Dorothy M. Horstmann, Eugene M. Waith, William Kessen, Harry R. Rudin, Edmund S. Morgan, Edwin McClellan, Edward S. Deevey, Jr., David Davis, Joseph LaPolombara, Robert Triffin, and Sidney W. Mintz. Also on the committee during that period were China historian Jonathan D. Spence and A. Bartlett Giamatti, a popular literature professor who was president of Yale from 1978 to 1986—the youngest president in the university's history—and commissioner of Major League Baseball from 1988 until his death a year later at the age of fifty-one.

John Ryden amplified on this development at a memorial address he gave in 1998 in honor of Ralph Brown, a professor at the Yale Law School for fifty years and a devoted champion of the Press who joined the Publications Committee in 1963 and was chairman from 1968 until he stepped down in 1981. "The PC, as it is always called, is one of Yale's most coveted committee assignments and has the reputation of being the university's best floating faculty seminar," Ryden said in his remarks, which were later reprinted in the *Yale Law Journal*. "Its members hold in their hands the imprint of the university, and they authorize its use *only* when books meet the university's highest standards and approach the ideals for which it stands. In other words, only when the books are good enough to carry the name 'Yale' on title page and spine."

Brown had a "long love affair" with the Press, Ryden said, and noted that the passion he had for its continued well-being began long before he joined the faculty. "To earn the money for his tuition at Yale Law School, Ralph worked on the Yale edition of *Horace Walpole's Letters*, a vast undertaking that took half a century and forty-eight volumes to complete, all made possible by the splendid beneficence of Wilmarth 'Lefty' Lewis. At the Walpole factory Ralph edited volumes nine and ten. Ralph's name appears under Lefty's on the title page; his work appears in the footnotes. The joke that swept the Graduate School that year was that Ralph's notes were more witty, erudite, and charming than the famously witty, erudite, and charming Horace Walpole himself."

Ryden said that by his count, Professor Brown had attended more than two hundred Publications Committee meetings, presiding over 150 of them, and in each instance helped make decisions that led to the publication of more than a thousand Yale books. "In the process he guided a succession of Yale scholars who then as now are more accustomed to guiding than to being guided. Veterans of the PC will tell you that there were two qualities that characterized Ralph's leadership. The first is that he was, above all, fair. The second is that he was a virtuoso at running meetings. Every book and every author got a fair hearing. All opinions were heard, and it all happened with apparent ease, no matter how long the agenda or how knotty the problem. He had an uncanny knack for finding consensus. Best of all, he made it fun."

TWO

The Middle Years

N 1949, A CONFEDERATION OF scholarly publishers established in common purpose just three years earlier issued the results of a detailed survey of their activities sponsored by the American Council of Learned Societies and funded by the Rockefeller Foundation. Titled *A Report on American University Presses,* the study was not occasioned by the observance of any milestone in particular, though it did amount to a reflection on the first seventy years or so of scholarly publishing in North America and offered the thirty-five members of the Association of American University Presses an opportunity to express, in a collegial way, what they felt was the role and mission of their endeavors. Widely quoted in professional circles in its day, the 302-page study came to be known as the Kerr Report for its author, a young Yale graduate named Chester Brooks Kerr, who would be hired by George

Parmly Day as secretary of Yale University Press shortly after the assessment was issued, an appointment due in no small measure to the approbation generated by his work on the survey and for the glowing words he had to say in its pages about the high-quality work being done in New Haven. Ten years after that, Kerr would succeed Norman V. Donaldson as director of the Press.

Of the thirty-five press directors Kerr interviewed for the study—and he made explicitly clear that his evaluation of the data went well beyond the dry examination of numbers and statistics to include personal contact with the principals—thirty-five different definitions of what constitutes a university press were assembled, a good number of which hold true today. "Some were very specific," Kerr wrote of the responses, "while others, like the hunters in *Peter and the Wolf*, came out shooting in all directions. Most were high-minded. Above all, there was a striking amount of fundamental agreement." Receiving special attention from Kerr was an excerpt from the address George Parmly Day delivered to a meeting of the Association of American Universities in Princeton, New Jersey, just six years after getting his own operation up and running at Yale. "The function of a university press," Day had declared in 1914, "is nothing less than to render distinct service to the world in general, through the medium of printing or publishing or both, and in such ways to supplement the work of education which commands the devotion of the university whose name it bears." That statement, Kerr concluded, had "satisfactorily met the test of time." In the penultimate paragraph to the report, Kerr called on his future employer once again for another salient observation: "Our American university presses have no propaganda to push, but in their lists are to be found many works which if widely read would give to our democracy the broad knowledge necessary for understanding and intelligent decision."

Not long after his report was published, Kerr told an interviewer for the trade journal *Publishers Weekly* that scholarly publishing is "the third function of the university, without which it is incomplete." The first function, he said, is the faculty, "for teaching and research." Then, he continued, comes the library, as a necessary "storehouse of knowledge.""To complete the act," he concluded, "you have to have the publishing house." Kerr shared a story of how the well-known bibliophile and noted Yale benefactor Wilmarth "Lefty" Lewis had once tried to make the same point to the renowned physicist J. Robert Oppenheimer; Lewis got nowhere with the concept, Kerr said, until he wrote on a blackboard: "Faculty + Library = Publication."

These days, the Kerr Report is not likely to find a wide audience outside the cozy world of academic publishing, but a close reading does give a sense of the author and, like his *Peter and the Wolf* comment, betrays periodic flashes of wry humor, a polished verbal touch that shows up every now and then in the minutes he wrote of board meetings during his years with the Press. More tellingly, it offers insight into the management style Kerr would employ when he was appointed director of Yale University Press, particularly in chapters he titled "Relations with the University" and "Relations with the Scholar" and in a closing section he called "Some Personal Opinions" that commented on changes and trends in the industry. On the matter of a scholarly press paying its own way, for instance, he offered this: "Over a period of years—and I cannot lay too much stress on the fact that it takes years—a press can increase its self-sufficiency, especially if it is skillfully managed."

Kerr expressed delicate praise for the clubby origins of the first American university presses while stressing an obvious need for greater discipline in the ranks and the hiring of capable staffs that would be directed by savvy professionals carefully schooled in the niceties of the business. "In the beginning," he wrote, "the motive power in university press publishing was supplied by a few far-sighted university administrators, energetic scholars, broad-minded librarians, enlightened alumni, and devoted practitioners of the art of printing, and the incentive provided by such individuals remains today one of the most valuable assets of a university press. Now, however, the moving power has passed into the hands of a new group of professionals, men and women dedicated to the aims of scholarship but also trained in the techniques of publishing."

It happened that these two key elements—skillful management ability and hands-on experience in the trade—were personal assets that Kerr must surely have highlighted in his résumé for the Yale job. After receiving his bachelor's degree from Yale in 1936—his roommate was an aspiring writer named John Hersey—Kerr began making his way in the publishing world, working variously as an editor at Harcourt, Brace and director of the newly formed Atlantic Monthly Press. During World War II, he served with the Office of War Information and the Bureau of Overseas Publications of the State Department as chief of the books department, responsible for producing pocket-sized editions of current literature known as the Armed Services Editions; some 123 million copies of 1,322 titles were produced over the life of the program. After the war, Kerr served as vice president of Reynal and Hitchcock, a New York publishing firm.

In the breezy reflection he wrote for the seventy-fifth birthday of the Press, Kerr was not shy about trumpeting the achievements of his twenty-year tenure as director. During the 1960s and 1970s—the years Kerr was in charge—the Press, he wrote, "grew steadily to new sizes. Its list rose from thirty titles a year to ninety—and the Yale Paperbounds became solidly entrenched as supplementary texts." Staff, meanwhile, increased to a complement of sixty men and women during his watch. "By the time Kerr retired in 1979," he wrote of himself, "the sales volume had multiplied ten times to top $4 million." During that span, Press headquarters had moved twice, in 1959 from the Governor Ingersoll House at 143 Elm Street to the old Bond Bakery building at 149 York Street, and from there fifteen years later to the charming accommodations it now occupies at 302 Temple Street. Most significant, perhaps, was the decision in 1961 to make the Press a department of the university, a unit responsible for its activities to the Yale Corporation through a Board of Governors, a move that Kerr hailed in his brief history as essential to its expanding role as a scholarly publisher. "Many saw this development," he wrote, "as a controlling link between the management of the Press and the administration of the University, and, more important, the beginning of a healthy new period in the role of the Press as a responsible organ of American scholarly publishing."

Indeed, the man who succeeded Kerr as director of the Press, John G. Ryden, stressed in his interview with me that one of his predecessor's singular achievements was the work he did in establishing this new relationship with the university. "Today, the Press is technically run by a Board of Governors which consists of the president and other senior officers of the university, a group of senior faculty, and several outsiders, all of whom are publishers, usually half a dozen of each, and the director is accountable to that board," he said. "Now, the president of the university, like a French king, could just get rid of the assembly if he wanted to, but he doesn't, and it's been a very good thing. It's something that Chester worked very hard to set up when the change was made, and it has provided a bit of a moat for the Press that has worked out quite satisfactorily ever since for all parties."

A vigorous, robust man who enjoyed wearing beautifully

tailored Savile Row suits, Chester Kerr, by all accounts, saw himself as the living symbol of the Press, a characterization that Ryden seconded with a hearty laugh when I asked him to describe his predecessor. "Oh, for sure," he agreed readily. "With Chester, it very definitely was the Press *c'est moi*. He was a tremendous presence, and maybe sometimes he did get in the way. He was a brilliant promoter, but he was promoting himself as much as the Press itself at any one time. Sometimes it was great for the Press, but sometimes it got in the way." Among his peers, Kerr enjoyed a sterling reputation, as suggested in an admiring profile of him written in 1976 for a newsletter issued by the Association of American University Publishers and published below a headline identifying him as the "stylish, scholarly 'godfather'" to university presses. "Disguising a lot of chutzpah beneath a languid old world charm, Kerr is central casting's dream of a scholarly publisher with his relaxed English tailoring and Anthony Eden mustache, all wreathed in the mellow fragrance of pipe tobacco."

Everyone interviewed for this retrospective agreed that Kerr had a swagger about him that tended to amuse his admirers and annoy his critics; for better or worse, nobody I spoke with was neutral on the man and his manner. "Chester was what you might call an imposing presence," was the way Marian Neal Ash, an editor at the Press for twenty-nine years, executive editor at the time of her retirement in 1989, put it. "Not only was he physically large, but when he came in your office, you were well aware that he was there."

Edmund S. Morgan, Sterling Professor of History Emeritus, was never employed by the Press but has had multiple dealings with it, as the author of a biography of Benjamin Franklin published in 2002 that has sold more than 120,000 copies in hardcover, as a member of the Governing Board of the Franklin Papers project, and as a member of the Publications Committee during much of the Kerr era. "Chester was so full of himself, but I had to admit that he certainly had style," Morgan told me one morning in his New Haven home. "He and Kingman Brewster were great friends, and that certainly didn't hurt his standing either," he added, a reference to the dynamic administrator who was president of Yale from 1963 to 1977. "What I mean by style," Morgan continued, "is something you can't really define. Chester regarded the Press as his personal domain, that's for sure. And if you do good things—as he certainly did—maybe that's all right. But he tended to run roughshod over people."

Morgan recalled one instance when he met with Kerr to discuss his decision to appoint William S. Wilcox to the Governing Board of the Franklin Papers project. Morgan had brought Wilcox in from the University of Michigan to direct the series as it entered the period when Benjamin Franklin was living in England, and wanted to make sure that he had a say on the board as well. "Bill Wilcox was an ideal choice for this period of Franklin's life," Morgan said. "I got the History Department to hire him part-time, and to be editor of the series. So I was talking to Chester about this—and, make no mistake, Chester considered the Franklin Papers *his* project —when the matter came up as to whether Bill should be on the board. Chester said, 'We *hired* him, didn't we?' I said, 'Chester, that's exactly what's wrong with you, and always has been. You think that the people who work for you are all hired hands. Forget it. I'm seeing to it that Bill is on the board.' And I did. In those days I had some muscle. But that's the kind of situation where I sometimes crossed swords with Chester. He rubbed a lot of people the wrong way." Morgan's assertion that Kerr regarded the Franklin series to be "his" project is reinforced by a charcoal portrait of the former director that hangs in the Press offices; it pictures a nattily dressed man in a smart blazer, puffing contentedly on a pipe. His arms are casually crossed, one over the other, a book firmly gripped in his left hand. The title, prominently facing outward: *The Papers of Benjamin Franklin.*

Tina C. Weiner, associate director and publishing director, has held a variety of positions since joining the Press in 1971 with a degree in art history from Smith College. Her impression of Kerr was that he had a "remarkable flair for publishing," and she praised him for "putting Yale Press on the map." Weiner said he "knew how to compete for publicity in the New York publishing world" and that she learned a lot from him on how to go about marketing and publicizing books, which became her specialty. "I will also say that he was mercurial and autocratic, and that he ran the Press as an old boys' club. Women were regularly paid less than their male counterparts, even if their performance was clearly superior." That said, she credited him with being "forward looking" in creating a London office and for laying the groundwork for the art and trade publishing programs. "He encouraged all of the editors to be innovative, and he encouraged me and my colleagues to build a more aggressive and creative marketing department."

Gaddis Smith, Larned Professor Emeritus of History at Yale and the author of numerous historical works, including a work in progress about Yale University in the twentieth century, had yet another perspective on Kerr and his way of doing business. "Chester was very creative and egocentric, a very funny guy," he told me. "He was just hilarious, a great wit. And he was very social. He lived in a big house on Humphrey Street, and he and his wife were renowned for their parties." Smith said he believed that Kerr's sense of humor may well have had something to do with the timing of the release of *The Vinland Map and the Tartar Relation,* one of the most controversial titles in the history of the Press and one that manages to stir debate among scholars to this day. That the news of the book's imminent publication attracted worldwide attention when it was announced was validation enough of Kerr's major-league approach to public relations, but the direction some of the stories took after the book began to circulate could not have been part of his original game plan.

The stated intention of the October 11, 1965, announcement was to declare, in a very splashy way, what was pro-

Wilhelmine Octavia Johnson Day (Mrs. George Parmly Day), c. 1903 *(Original the property of Mr. and Mrs Day; copied by Harold Shapiro for the Press, 1958)*

George Parmly Day, founder and director of Yale University Press, 1908–1944

Title page of the first edition
of the first book published by
Yale University Press, in 1909

The Ginn Building,
70 Fifth Avenue, New York,
where the Press set up shop
in 1908 *(Engraving: Jon
DePol)*

The printing office at
149 York Street, c. 1960
(Photo: A. Burton Street)

The shipping room
at 149 York Street, c. 1960
(Photo: A. Burton Street)

Chester Kerr, director of
Yale University Press,
1959–1979

Carl Purington Rollins, printer emeritus to the university, inspects a new offset press with Alvin Eisenman, adviser to the Press on typography, c. 1960 *(Photo: A. Burton Street)*

A one-ton package containing the one-millionth pound of paper to be used by Yale University Press for its paperbound book list is shipped in 1964 by Carter Rice Storrs and Bemet. Pictured at the Carl Purington Rollins Printing Office are Joseph Pongonis, head pressman of the Press; Edwin Benedict (with glasses), assistant pressman; and, reading from back to front: Donald B. Page, Carter Rice sales representative; Robert H. Hennings, Yale University Press plant manager; and Karl Reugkert, plant superintendent *(Photo: Yale Office of Public Affairs)*

The Vinland Map and Chester Kerr, 1965

Frank M. Turner

The London office,
47 Bedford Square, Bloomsbury
(Photo: Nicholas A. Basbanes)

John Nicoll, director of the
London office, 1973–2003
(Photo: Nicholas A. Basbanes)

Yale University Press Publications Committee, 1982–1983. *Clockwise from far end of table:* John Ryden, Albert Solnit, Edward Tripp, Georges May, Charles Grench, C. Vann Woodward, Maureen MacGrogan, Ralph Brown, Jaroslav Pelikan (chairman), Marian Neal Ash, Ellen Graham, Martin Klein, Judy Metro, Gladys Topkis, and Robert Handschumacher. *Not pictured:* James Scott *(Photo: David Ottenstein)*

claimed at the time to be clear and convincing proof that the
first European voyager to visit North America was not Christopher Columbus in 1492 but the eleventh-century Viking
seafarer Leif Eriksson, big news indeed by any measurement.
Giving the story an extra push was the fact that the Press had
kept all details of the scholarly project secret before announcing its publication a day before thousands of Italian Americans would celebrate Columbus Day throughout the United
States, a circumstance many observers considered less than
coincidental. Newspapers on both sides of the Atlantic found
the assertion irresistible, not least among them the *New York
Times,* which featured the story on its front page beneath a
three-column headline that read "1440 Map Depicts the New
World." The *Times* spread included a reproduction of the map
outlining, in strikingly accurate detail, Iceland, Greenland,
and the northeast coast of what we know today as North
America, or Vinland, as it is identified on the chart. Adding
weight to the visual evidence were two explanatory inscrip-
tions, known as legends, written on the map in Latin that
seemed to document the sensational claims in unequivocal
terms—and they were put there, it was argued, by an unknown
scribe half a century before Columbus set sail on the *Santa
Maria,* copied, it was suggested, from some earlier, now lost,
source.

The ramifications of all this were best expressed by a
group of Yale scholars, who described the document as nothing less than "the most exciting cartographic discovery of the

century." Drawn in brown ink on parchment, the eleven-
by-sixteen-inch chart had come to light eight years earlier
bound in a volume that also included a manuscript account
of a papal mission in 1245–1247 to the land of the Mongols,
or Tartars as they were called by Christians at that time, by
a Franciscan traveler known as Friar John of Plano Carpini.
The only connection between the map and the account of the
thirteenth-century prelate's journey to the Far East was that
both had been secured in the same leather binding. The two
documents had been acquired in 1957 by Laurence C. Witten II, a rare-book dealer based in New Haven, from Enso
Ferrajoli de Ry, an Italian book scout living in Barcelona,
Spain, through the Swiss dealer Nicolas Rauch, for $3,500. An
anonymous benefactor subsequently bought the map for Yale
for an unconfirmed price reported in one published account
to be $300,000; thirty years later, the great Yale philanthropist
Paul Mellon would be identified as the generous donor.

James Tanis, the university librarian at the time, called
the Vinland Map "the most exciting single acquisition of the
Yale Library in modern times, exceeding in significance even
Yale's Gutenberg Bible and Bay Psalm Book." Alexander O.
Vietor, Yale's curator of maps and one of the scholars who had
been allowed to study the crinkly document, boldly declared it
to be "the greatest treasure of the Yale Map collection," an archive that includes among its storehouse of rarities the famed
Henricus Martellus map of 1489, a benchmark rendering that
depicts the world as it was known to Europeans just before

Columbus embarked on his first voyage of discovery three years later. Vietor's authentication was seconded by Raleigh A. Skelton, superintendent of maps in the British Museum; George D. Painter, assistant keeper in charge of incunabula in the British Museum's Department of Printed Books; and Thomas E. Marston, curator of medieval and Renaissance manuscripts at Yale.

Beyond the sensational claim itself was the matter of the timing. "New Haven at the time was reputed to have the highest percentage of people with Italian origin of any city outside of Italy," Gaddis Smith told me. "The mayor, a good number of our mayors, have been Italian; the world headquarters of the Knights of Columbus is here, pizza in America began here on Wooster Street at Frank Pepe's and Sally's. So the people around here were pretty angry, and Chester Kerr said, 'Oh, it was just a coincidence.' Well, I never believed that for a minute." If the backlash had been restricted to local anger, the story might not have generated the kind of traction it did, but the indignation went well beyond New Haven. John N. LaCorte, president of the Italian Historical Society of America, said flatly on the day of the announcement that he and his colleagues were going "to put Yale University against the wall." Among public figures to pick up on the story was the comedian Jimmy Durante, who joked that although he was not "poissonally" acquainted with Columbus, he was certain that when the explorer arrived in America, he "played only to Indians—there were no Norwegians in the audience." John

Lindsay, Yale Class of 1944 and LLB 1948, a congressman who was then a candidate for mayor of New York, a city with a rich Italian-American constituency, said that "to say Columbus didn't discover America is as absurd as saying DiMaggio doesn't know anything about baseball or that Toscanini and Caruso weren't great musicians."

Kerr, meanwhile, was adamant that the date of the announcement was dictated by the vicissitudes of production schedules and was not the eager exploitation of a public relations opportunity. "We planned to publish the book in the spring, but there was a delay in getting the proofs read, which meant it couldn't come out until June," he insisted in a 1968 interview, an explanation he repeated on numerous occasions in later years. "I didn't want it to get lost in the summer, light-reading season, so we decided to wait until the fall." At first, Kerr maintained, the book was to be announced on October 9, declared that year by President Lyndon Johnson as a national day of recognition for Leif Eriksson, but since October 9 in 1965 fell on a Saturday—a very slow news cycle—the following Monday was selected. "That was where I made my great mistake," Kerr allowed. "I was always accused of doing this deliberately to discredit Columbus in favor of Leif Eriksson, but the truth is that it was a complete accident."

The first mention of *The Vinland Map* to appear in the minutes of the Publications Committee came on February 18, 1963, with Kerr informing his colleagues that "an exciting manuscript will shortly be presented to the Press: an unnamed collector associated with Yale has acquired an early pre-Columbian map of the Western world that shows promise of being one of the most historical cartographic discoveries of recent years. A manuscript of 40,000 words assessing the map has been written by R. A. Skelton, Keeper of Maps of the British Museum, and contributions to the book will be made by George Painter, Thomas Marston, and, possibly, Alexander Vietor." Two months later, the committee was advised that "1440 can be confirmed" as a probable date of composition for the map, "and that the Press should welcome submission of the manuscript." On March 11, 1964—seven months before publication—Kerr was predicting a "bumper crop" for the fall list, "probably the strongest ever brought out by the Press in one season, headed as it is by *The Vinland Map and the Tartar Relation,* a scholarly presentation of two of the most remarkable acquisitions ever made by the Yale Library."

The cartographic coup, of course, rated top billing, but Kerr was pleased to single out in his presentation other high-profile books that would be appearing on the list along with it, and they demonstrate, in a snap-shot kind of way, what a typical Yale University Press list had come to represent in the years approaching its fiftieth birthday. The forthcoming releases included: René Dubos, *Man Adapting;* William K. Wimsatt, *The Portraits of Alexander Pope;* R. W. B. Lewis, *Trials of the Word: Essays in American Literature and the Humanistic Tradition;* Charles Seymour, *Letters from the Paris Peace Conference;* W. Turrentine Jackson, *Wagon Roads West: A Study of Federal*

*Road Surveys and Construction in the Trans-Mississippi West,
1846–1869;* and William Stevenson Smith, *Interconnections in
the Ancient Near-East: A Study of the Relationships between
the Arts of Egypt, the Aegean, and Western Asia.* Four other
authors cited at that meeting by Kerr, and their books—Colin
McPhee, *Music in Bali: A Study in Form and Instrumental Organization in Balinese Orchestral Music;* Carroll L. V. Meeks,
Italian Architecture, 1750–1914; Marshall D. Shulman, *Beyond
the Cold War;* and Robert Ignatius Burns, S.J., *The Jesuits and
the Indian Wars of the Northwest*—would be delayed, and appeared in 1966; another, *The Historical World of Frederick Jackson
Turner, with Selections from His Correspondence,* by Wilbur R.
Jacobs, was issued in 1968.

Similarly, there were no provocative titles or controversial news reports to discuss at the May 18, 1964, meeting
of the Publications Committee either, where a number of
other scholarly works were also approved, including *Scales and
Weights: A Historical Outline,* by Bruno Kisch, the first volume
of a new series in the History of Science and Medicine. In
other business that day, Leonard Labaree's volume 8 of *The
Papers of Benjamin Franklin* "was accepted without question,"
and William G. Shepherd's *Economic Performance under Public
Ownership: British Fuel and Power,* the latest installment in the
Yale Studies in Economics, was approved, along with Linda
Hsia's *Speak Chinese: Supplementary Materials.* But what makes
the minutes of this meeting unusually interesting, coming as
it does eighteen months before *The Vinland Map* would domi-

nate most public discussion of Yale University Press, is the lengthy discussion it summarizes under the heading of "New Manuscripts—General," a philosophical debate, it turned out, on the merits of taking on a book with the rather daunting title of *Microscopic Diagnosis of the Parasites of Man*, submitted by Dr. Robert B. Burrows, an eminent epidemiologist. The principal thrust of the committee's concern was "what Press policy should be in regard to a laboratory tool of this kind. The majority opinion was that if the book could be characterized as ground-breaking, important in its field, and so limited in its sales as not to appeal to a commercial publisher—all of which appeared to be true of the Burrows book—the Press would be performing a service by bringing it out." The book was accepted for publication and issued the following year. It was pretty much business as usual at a meeting of the Publications Committee on December 6, 1965, too, with the happy announcement that of 240 books selected in the November 25, 1965, issue of the *Times Literary Supplement* (London) as being the "most important American books published in the last five years," twenty-seven titles—better than 10 percent—had been issued by Yale, a remarkable showing.

Just a month before *The Vinland Map and the Tartar Relation* would be announced to the world, Kerr shared with his colleagues the "cheerful news" that the previous year's sales "were the highest in the history of the Press, and the first two months of the fiscal year indicate that 1965–66 will break the present record." Along with the robust sales figures was the disclosure that the book "with the highest selling price ever assigned" by the Press to an individual title, two hundred dollars for *Interaction of Color*, by Josef Albers, was about to sell out its run; the book had been issued in a limited edition of two hundred copies featuring 150 silkscreen color plates, and despite the high demand for the book—it sold out within months of its release—production costs were much too high to justify reprinting in hardcover. The book had taken eight years to prepare, weighed twenty-two pounds, and was declared an instant classic. Whenever copies show up on the antiquarian market today, they typically command five-figure prices, heady validation of its enduring importance—but nothing, certainly, to occasion front-page coverage by the world press.

Monday, October 11, 1965, on the other hand, began with the banner headline in the *New York Times*, and the news only got more exhilarating as the day progressed. The minutes of a noon luncheon meeting of the Publications Committee recount how Kerr, "fresh from presenting a copy of *The Vinland Map and the Tartar Relation* to the King of Norway, reported on the haps and mishaps of his trip there and to England on behalf of the book. Cables received from both London and Oslo during the lunch said that television, radio, and newspaper coverage was at that moment enormous." A dinner and reception was scheduled later in the day, he continued, "to launch in this country one of the most exciting and potentially important books to issue from a university press in many years." At 3:30 p.m., the Governing Board met in the George Parmly Day Memorial Room at Press headquarters, then 149 York Street. After dispensing with the formalities, Kerr got to the meat of the meeting, with news that simultaneous publication was being planned for *The Vinland Map* in England and Norway. "Reviewers, newspaper reporters, and scholars in both countries, as well as in the United States, have been briefed and the size of the news break is already apparent," he enthused, and once again referred to himself in the third person: "Whether all the attention to the story of the Map's discovery and documentation will result in increased distribution for the book remains to be seen, but while Mr. Kerr was talking he was handed a message requesting him to telephone the Book-of-the-Month Club after the meeting." The board adjourned at 5:00 p.m. "to permit members to dress for the dinner to be given jointly by the Press and the Library in celebration of the acquisition and publication of *The Vinland Map and the Tartar Relation*." The Book-of-the-Month Club would announce a few weeks later that it had indeed selected *The Vinland Map* as a dividend selection for its members, the fourth time a Yale book had been so designated (the first was a facsimile edition of the First Folio of Shakespeare, the second was The Yale Shakespeare, the third was *Long Day's Journey into Night*).

Ebullience continued at the November 9 meeting of the Publications Committee, though a mild note of discord was expressed by Kerr, who offhandedly mentioned that the triumphant release of *The Vinland Map* "had been somewhat marred by the grumblings of certain faculty scholars who felt that they should have been informed in advance by the Library curators of the work in progress or even consulted; some of those complaining were made additionally unhappy at not being invited to the publication day reception. Mr. Kerr expressed the Press's regret over any such omissions. In every other way the publication has been an uproarious success despite wrathful denunciations of the timing by Italian-American groups." It was further reported that the Rand McNally Company had been authorized to market individual copies of the map "suitable for framing," with the caveat that they were intended "primarily for institutional use." At the December 10 meeting, Kerr reported that the "spectacular success" of the book had "contributed hugely to autumn revenues," with sales having already reached eight thousand copies, "despite the long out-of-stock periods which followed the initial reception so unexpectedly." The Book-of-the-Month Club and the History Book Club accounted for an additional twenty-five thousand copies in print. A month later, Kerr would be reporting that the book continued "to fill our coffers despite a running fire from the Italians. The Library shares in the windfall, having accumulated royalties of $12,000 by the end of December."

All was not well in the scholarly world, however, and a barrage of criticism that had been mounted in some quarters began to take its toll. At a 1966 conference convened by the

Smithsonian Institution, lingering doubts about the map's authenticity prompted Yale to commission an independent laboratory to reexamine it. New X-rays disclosed the presence of a crystalline form of titanium dioxide known as anatase; rarely encountered in nature, the mineral was not produced commercially as a white pigment until 1920. It was on the strength of these findings that Sterling Memorial Library officials announced in January 1974 that "the famous Vinland Map may be a forgery."

Over at the Press, meanwhile, the book was allowed to go out of print. Twenty years later, however, yet another series of independent experiments and studies concluded that the map might be authentic after all, with a pair of scientists arguing that anatase could possibly have been used in the making of a medieval ink. This prompted the publication of a new edition in 1995 that added updated reports on the continuing controversy, including an account from Laurence Witten on how he had acquired the document in the first place, an intriguing explanation since the issue of provenance before World War II remained unresolved. There also was a "Note from the Publisher," signed jointly by Chester Kerr as director emeritus and his successor, John Ryden, that gave a summary account of the brouhaha. It was in this two-page overview that Paul Mellon was identified as the donor, reported with the added detail that the greatest benefactor in Yale history had made the gift on the condition that it first be authenticated by reputable scholars. It was also disclosed that Mellon and the widow of Alexander Vietor had underwritten publication costs of the second edition. Significantly, Kerr and Ryden were careful about making daring claims, as their final words make clear: "We can only hope that this new edition will lead to the rehabilitation of one of history's most important cartographical finds, which has too long languished under a cloud."

Ryden was more pointed in an interview with Jennifer Kaylin of the *Yale Alumni Magazine*. "To the extent possible, the people involved have been vindicated," he told her. "All the apparently damning evidence was overturned, which led us to conclude that the map had received a bum rap." He added his measured belief that scholars and scientists can never say with complete assurance that an artifact is genuine. "You can never prove authenticity, you can only disprove it. Secretly, I feel that to leave a little bit of mystery is probably a good thing."

In hindsight, it can be argued that the initial publication of the map resulted from a logical conjunction of circumstances perfectly suited to the mission of a university press, one involving the study and interpretation of a unique manuscript that is a prize possession of the university it serves. That another group of experts would declare the map to be a clever deception two years later is not really the salient point in this context, since serious inquiry had been conducted in good faith beforehand and reputable authorities had endorsed the project. Whether the publication of a second edition in 1995 was warranted is arguable, but the document itself remains a matter of continuing contention, as evidenced by the release in 2004 of *Maps, Myths, and Men: The Story of the Vinland Map*, in which Kirsten A. Seaver, a fellow of the Royal Carto-graphic Society of London, put forth the name of Father Josef Fischer (1858–1944), a German Jesuit scholar renowned for his grasp of Norse geography and history, as the puta-tive forger. In 1974, two Yale professors, Robert S. Lopez and Konstantin Reichardt, had proposed the name of a Dalmatian Franciscan friar, Luka Jelic (1863–1922), of the Seminary at Zadar, Yugoslavia, as the likely culprit. Like all other hypoth-eses involving this document, nothing is certain, nothing is conclusive, and readers who wish for more detail are advised to consult the numerous articles and monographs that have been published on the matter over the years, and decide for themselves. From a publishing standpoint, at least, the saga of the Vinland Map was an edifying episode in the life of an American university press.

Another opportunity for Kerr to make headlines would present itself in 1971, this time with the chance to publish an inside account of a British intelligence coup that had been declared off-limits in the United Kingdom since the end of World War II but was fair game elsewhere. The book, titled *The Double-Cross System in the War of 1939 to 1945*, was writ-ten by Sir John Cecil Masterman, an Oxford historian who had worked for British military intelligence during the war as chairman of what was known as the Twenty Committee. The elite group included key personnel from the academic community and had supervised an ingenious program of counterespionage to turn a network of German spies into double agents. Called the Double Cross System, the name of the operation was based on the Roman numerals XX for the number of members in the Twenty Committee and was a visual pun that suggested its turnabout-is-fair-play reason for being. As the institutional historian of the operation, Masterman was eager to publish the account he had written of its activities, especially when bits and pieces of its spectacular success began appearing in other publications in the late 1960s. After the British government rebuffed repeated attempts to declassify the narrative under provisions of the Official Secrets Act, Masterman was introduced to Chester Kerr by Norman Holmes Pearson, a former wartime colleague of his who was then a professor of English and American studies at Yale.

By now Masterman was provost of Worcester College and vice-chancellor of Oxford, and he liked the idea of signing on with a distinguished university press, especially one that had an active division in London that could distribute his book in Europe. Another factor that contributed to Masterman's decision to publish with Yale, according to Robin W. Winks in *Cloak and Gown: Scholars in the Secret War, 1939–1961,* was Kerr's reputation as someone "noted for his interest in Britain, his shrewd business judgment, his willingness to do battle, and his imaginative list." Kerr, in turn, offered Masterman a five-thousand-dollar advance for the manuscript, an "unprecedented" sum for a scholarly publisher. The book, Winks wrote, became "an instant classic of espionage and intelligence," selling forty-five thousand copies in hardcover, two hundred thousand in paperback, and thousands more in German, Italian, Portuguese, and Swedish translation. In his preface, Masterman wrote that he never entertained any thoughts of publication when he prepared the report in 1945, but circumstances changed. "As the secrets of the war years were revealed the objections to publication steadily diminished, for it can now be argued that nothing which could be of value to a potential enemy is revealed which is not already known."

For all the zest he had for big books such as *The Vinland Map* and *The Double-Cross System,* Kerr remained firm in his commitment to be a champion of the scholarly monograph, according to Marian Ash. "When I first came to the Press in 1959, we never considered the cost or the potential market, or what we would make from a book," she told me one morning in 2005, seated in her former office on the second floor of 302 Temple Street for the first time since her retirement seventeen years earlier. "I can remember Chester standing in my office, right over there, and saying, 'As long as I am director of the Press, we will not take into account the potential sales of a manuscript before taking it on.'" She quickly acknowledged that "this was the good old days" and that Kerr "changed" as time went on and as demands to balance his budgets became more pressing. "Another editor and I once observed at a university press meeting that Princeton, particularly, was pretty good at estimating in advance the number of copies they would sell and how many they would have to print. So we made up a little form of our own that took these kinds of projections into account. When I showed that to Chester, he said, 'We are not going, to be so'—well, he didn't say *crass*, but that was the meaning." Kerr was not difficult to work with, Ash said, "but he did want his own way, and I will say this—he very much respected editors. In fact, he never, almost never, read our manuscripts. An occasional art book, maybe, but I can't ever remember him reading a manuscript. And the truth is, I'd rather have a director who didn't read manuscripts. He gave us a lot of freedom, and very often if we had a disagreement with some other department, he would take the editor's side. We had to approve the design of the book, and if there was something we didn't like about it, our word would carry great weight. If it was design versus editor, he felt pretty much the editor was right."

Kerr was respected throughout the publishing industry as a complete bookman, and if he delegated the reading of manuscripts to others, the probable reason, as Ash suggested, was because he trusted the judgment of his staff. When Kerr took over the Houghton Mifflin imprint of Ticknor and Fields following his retirement from Yale in 1979, one of his chief joys, he told the *New York Times,* was the opportunity he had to dip into manuscripts. "At Yale I was removed from the editorial process," he said. "We had a staff of 60—six were editors—and we published 90 books a year. Here we are only 11, and I'm back reading manuscripts and forming the initial judgments. We can act quickly, too. At a university press, books get bogged down by the number of people who must read them or in the committee meetings where decisions are made."

Kerr shared several observations gleaned from having spent so many years directing a scholarly press and applying what he learned to his new life back in commercial publishing, where he had begun his career. "Many publishers are drawing in their horns on trade books," he said, describing books that today might be described as "mid-list" titles with moderate expectations of sales. "They funnel their activity on the best sellers. Everyone's looking for books to sell to paperback or film for hundreds of thousands of dollars. This limits opportunities for authors and deprives readers as well. When Houghton Mifflin decided to expand trade publications they had two choices: expand their present operation by adding more editors, or striking out with a new subsidiary, which would have new blood and new attitudes." The "new blood and new attitudes," of course, were those of Chester Kerr, and he made clear his intention to think broadly and to be something other than "solely a literary imprint." He stressed a goal of "looking for books with a long life, not just those that make one big splash. I think it's still possible to publish books of quality with a sufficient market and to have the agility to sell subsidiary rights to a point where we can stay out of bankruptcy. It's most gratifying that at this moment there's a growing recognition of our existence and books of that sort are coming to us from agents and authors. But you can't sit there and wait. We've taken the initiative to find people to write the kinds of books we feel are needed."

There came a point in the mid-1960s, Marian Ash recalled, when there was a change in attitude around the Press. "We had moved into these fancy quarters over on York Street, very modern, and the offices were very nice. The editors had a whole separate area, and we were behind glass, with nice new furniture. Right away, it was clear that something had changed in the Press, and Chester was interested in everything we did. It was never the kind of pressure that may have kept you awake at night, wondering 'How can I do so much work?' But we all worked very hard, and I think we all knew Chester was anxious to build up the Press to become even more an institution of prestige. He was very active in the university press association, in fact he served as president at one time, and I think we all kind of caught that spirit of becoming better than we were, and bigger. And I guess one of the reasons was that suddenly there was more money available for more books."

The source of all this money, Ash said, came by way of what was known at the time as the New Math, a popular phrase used to describe an ambitious teaching program developed in the 1960s by an organization known as the School Mathematics Study Group (SMSG) and financed by the National Science Foundation. The effort was created in 1958 in response to the Soviet Union's early triumphs in the space race, notably the launching a year earlier of Sputnik, the world's first satellite. In an almost frantic attempt to create a new generation of scientists and engineers who would return the United States to technological superiority, SMSG was tasked with developing new mathematics curricula for primary and secondary education, an undertaking it pursued through 1977. The program culminated in a series of books prepared entirely by its staff and issued at first by Yale, later by Random House, and distributed to schools nationwide, with the federal government picking up the tab. "We were publishing the New Math, and getting all kinds of money for doing it, with practically no expenses," Ash said. "That was a kind of separate operation, and I never had anything to do with it, but we were all aware that it was a driving little industry in there, and as I say, it was fairly common knowledge that it financed the growth of the Press. So that if there were no questions raised—let's say I had three books for one season, and the next season I had five—nobody said, 'Oh, we can't afford to do them.' And I think Chester set the figure—I think he wanted to go up to fifty books a year by some point—so we were all trying to meet that goal."

Minutes of various Press meetings from the period give a degree of specificity to Ash's recollections. At a May 22, 1964, meeting of the Governing Board, Kerr offered "a financial report for the nine months ending March 21, showing that the Press is on its way to a record year in publishing sales and that thanks to the SMSG income it has been able to meet the necessary increases in operating costs and inventory investment which have accompanied this growth." Kerr noted further that the "SMSG sets," as they were described, "continue to sell very well indeed and a total of over 900,000 will be sold in the fiscal year," as compared with 730,000 the previous year. And the number of new books issued each season, as Marian Ash had recalled, kept growing as a consequence. In 1958–1959, the Press released forty-five hardcover titles; by 1963–1964—during the years of the New Math windfall—the list had grown to fifty-eight titles; the following year it increased yet again to seventy-five.

At a May 17, 1968, meeting of the Governing Board, Kerr presented some summary numbers of the six-year collaboration just concluding, noting that total sales had amounted to about $7 million, of which $2 million "was returned to the National Science Foundation as sheer profit," with $666,000 "assigned to Yale Press as service charges." One of the board members, Arthur Rosenthal, "asked if another SMSG-like arrangement was in prospect; Mr. Kerr said that, unhappily, there was none, for commercial publishers were taking up this kind of experimental project that they had shied away from five years ago." Five months later, the precise figures for the enterprise would be itemized in a final report. Gross receipts for sales received by Yale came to $7.2 million. Manufacturing costs had amounted to $3.6 million, with another $808,000 received for warehousing and shipping. An additional "overhead charge" of $665,463 was assessed as well. Kerr wrote in the minutes that there was "full agreement" among the Governing Board members "that the project was a welcome contribution in which all concerned came out ahead: the books were published well, the National Science Foundation received a large sales income which it could use for further projects, and the Press was able to make good use of its income from the project."

Another distinguished Yale educator and author with recollections from this period, Jonathan Spence, recalled his experiences with Kerr with equanimity. "I came to Yale as a student in 1959, and when I joined the faculty in 1965, Chester invited me to come on the Publications Committee. It was a great committee, and very exciting. We read a lot, and we argued and talked a lot about books. It was just very stimulating." Named Sterling Professor of History at Yale in 1993, Spence published his first book, *Ts'ao Yin and the K'ang-hsi Emperor: Bondservant and Master*, with the Press in 1966, but after that he wrote mainly for trade presses, Little, Brown, Alfred A. Knopf, and Viking among them. As a person who has had extensive experience in both worlds—commercial and scholarly publishing—Spence said he admired Kerr as "a kind of publishing visionary, a perfectionist," who had "very strong views of how Yale might create a world-class university press. He'd had publishing experience, and he'd had strong connections with Yale. My memory of Chester Kerr is largely just of him going for quality, wanting to make sure that inadequate books were not slipping into the system, that his own staff would really read carefully the manuscripts that were coming in. And also that they would try and decide not just on the basis of current senior faculty handing in a manuscript, though he felt that was important, to keep Yale's faculty publishing with the Press. My point is that you both try and get the local faculty, and you try and really scan the world of learning out there to see what is new and important. I think Chester had a sense of where great strengths might lie. And I think history was one of them, English literature was one of them, the great collections. And he was a huge supporter of the Younger Poets Series. So Chester was just enormously lively. But he also exasperated people. He saw himself in a continuity of fine publishers. I think he wanted to have the best press in the States. I don't think he was a modest man. As soon as the British arts center came into being, he saw the possibilities of linkage there. But it wasn't inevitable. It needed somebody to make the decision to really begin thinking how we might publish great art books that would also be academically very strong."

Indeed, what is roundly praised as one of Kerr's masterstrokes was his decision to set up a London division that went well beyond being a business office that flies the flag abroad, so to speak, but has no role in the acquisition, editing, or production of books. Many American scholarly presses routinely print on the title pages of their books a line of type suggesting that the work has been issued jointly in two cities, the first typically being the location of the university itself, the second, almost without exception, London. While this certainly projects a cosmopolitan character, what it actually means, as a practical matter, is that the press maintains a sales office in the United Kingdom, with foreign rights to various titles being negotiated there. Though a bit misleading—it does bear some resemblance to the padding of a curriculum vitae—there is certainly nothing overly deceptive or irregular about this practice; it is, basically, what it is, however disingenuous it may seem to some sensibilities.

In the instance of Yale, there is not only a London office but a full-fledged editorial operation that accounts for about 40 percent of the titles produced under the Yale imprint, Robert Baldock, the director of the division, told me one March morning in 2006. We met in the elegant offices the Press maintains in an eighteenth-century Georgian house at 47 Bedford Square in Bloomsbury, an ideal setting in a literary district for the overseas headquarters of a distinguished American publisher. Three years earlier, Baldock had succeeded John Nicoll, the man widely credited with making the satellite operation the remarkable success it is today. In some ways the London office represents another example of an opportunity recognized, and an opportunity seized, and as Jonathan Spence indicated in his interview with me, "it wasn't inevitable."

Every university press has a mission statement to explain its reason for being, and though there is a degree of uniformity

in a lot of what each one says about itself and its goals—
seriousness in purpose, making contributions to the world of
knowledge, and promoting the goals of scholarship are among
the most often stated—there are shadings in nuance. Not surprisingly, many scholarly presses specialize in the history, art,
environment, economy, and culture of their geographic regions
as a matter of civic responsibility, publishing worthwhile books
that might otherwise never see the light of day and enhanc-
ing their commitment to their host communities. Even Yale
University Press pays occasional attention to its immediate
surroundings, the most consequential example, perhaps, the
publication in 1961 of *Who Governs?* a penetrating evaluation
of various power structures in the city of New Haven—some
formal, some informal, some overt, some covert—written by
the eminent Yale political scientist Robert Dahl as a case study
of the theoretical concept known as pluralism. But that kind of
monograph is the exception, and by no means the rule, since
the Press openly regards itself as a university press with no
physical limitations whatsoever, a point it states unequivocally
in its "vision" declaration for the twenty-first century, noting
that by maintaining an "international office in London," it is
able to implement its work "in a truly global manner." Yale
University Press, Limited—the name was changed to Yale
University Press, London, in 1984—was established in July
1961 for the modest purpose of selling abroad books produced
in New Haven through a consortium that included several
other American university presses. For the next nine years

that arrangement continued uneventfully, and it could well still be the case today were it not for the emergence of what became an untenable situation involving the university. In 1970, the Paul Mellon Centre for Studies in British Art was established in London, an extraordinary undertaking underwritten by the late Paul Mellon. One of the functions of the center was to prepare and publish serious scholarship about British art, a responsibility that by all anecdotal accounts did not go well at first.

"The short of the matter is that it was hemorrhaging money," John Ryden told me matter-of-factly. John Nicoll used somewhat different imagery to describe the dilemma, but the sentiment he expressed over a two hour London lunch with me was the same. "They were gushing money like it was water, and I can actually put some numbers on it, because they did a huge book in 1971 on William Hogarth, two volumes, and they spent seventy thousand pounds to print three thousand copies of it, which would be about a million pounds today, perhaps a bit more. It's almost inconceivable that this could have happened, but it did. The book was set in hot metal, it was done in Holland, it was all done very decently, to be sure. But they were spending this money at a prodigious rate, and Paul Mellon's lawyers told them to rein it in, and the way they did this was to fold it back into the museum he was building in New Haven, and the university took on the obligation to run the Mellon Centre."

In agreeing to do this, the university assumed responsibility to make good on a number of publishing commitments the Mellon Centre had already made to produce additional books. "This obligation was passed on to the Press by the university, and the Press, being good citizens, said 'Okay, we'll do them,'" Nicoll continued. "What Chester didn't realize at the time was that these books would involve someone in New Haven having to deal with some fairly ambitious, difficult, opinionated Brits, so the first two or three titles produced out of New Haven were not significantly more successful in terms of economy, and certainly not in terms of efficiency, than the ones that had been done previously by the foundation. So Chester then decided, rightly, that the only way to handle this was to produce the books in the U.K. After a bit of groping back and forth, Chester finally hired me, I suspect to solve a political problem that he had gotten into in New Haven on this very sensitive matter. He was anxious that the Mellon lawyers not get too twitchy—things had to be done to keep them happy—so in 1973 he brought me in, and it was for the specific purpose of doing these books."

At the time Nicoll had been employed by the Clarendon Press of Oxford University Press and was looking to make a move. "Oxford was a complete shambles in the sixties," he said. "It was run like an Oxford college, entirely in the interest of the fellows, and Chester knew I was disenchanted with all of that. So I was ready to leave. But he interviewed me just for these three or four art books that they were obligated to do. I said, 'Well, that is never going to make a publishing list, just a few books about British art,' and so I asked him, 'Can I do other books as well?' And he said, 'Yes, you can do any books that are appropriate for a university press.' I'd been doing art history books at Oxford, a little bit of literature, but in effect he gave me carte blanche to publish an academic list—any academic list that I could reasonably sort of justify. Up to that time, all the Yale office in London was doing was selling New Haven's books in Europe. And Yale had always had a strong English list—Yale has always been strongly Anglocentric —so I had a great deal of latitude to do what I wanted. I was luckier than I realized." Nicoll told me he had "heard all the stories" about Kerr over the years, and he felt a degree of sympathy with a number of his colleagues, particularly those who worked in the same building with him every day, under his watchful eye. "As the female staff in New Haven would have children, he'd say, 'They think they invented mother-hood.' He was an amazing guy, actually. But truth be told, I had a very considerable affection for him. Yes, he could behave very badly, and he was very selfish and ruthless when he wanted to be. But I was very lucky; I managed to stay on the right side of him."

Once he had Kerr's backing to build his own list, Nicoll proceeded to distinguish himself with a line of intelligently conceived and exquisitely produced books encompassing various aspects of the fine arts, the history of art and architecture, and social history, a specialty that grew and blossomed well beyond the Kerr years and continues to distinguish Yale

University Press. Not only did he take a direct hand in commissioning works and editing manuscripts, he supervised every aspect of production, selecting printing operations throughout the world that met his exacting standards. The secret to making these books so outstanding, according to John Ryden, who worked productively with the London office throughout his own tenure as director of the Press from 1979 to 2002, was Nicoll's insistence on quality bookmaking. "He was very shrewd and very smart, and he was very, very savvy," Ryden said. "You cannot tell the story of the Yale University Press in the last thirty-odd years without talking about London. It was terribly important, and for a good while it was the Press's cash cow. It was turning back money to New Haven largely through the art publishing program, which allowed us to reinvest again and to grow. John was a very big part of that. He's a great publisher. There is no other American university press that has anything like it at all. The fact that Yale has this major arm that is itself a great publishing company—and it is thought of that way, I might say, throughout the industry—is quite remarkable. And now all the art books that come out of New Haven follow his model as well."

Nicoll was genuinely amused when I related John Ryden's "cash cow" observation to him, not because he disagreed with it in any way, but for the fact that anyone from New Haven would acknowledge the circumstance in such a frank and open manner. "They'll say so now," he said, "but they would never admit it at the time. I knew it, but nobody else did. No one else in New Haven would admit it because they didn't think in those terms, and nobody said it in public. Ever. I'm amused that they would say it now. Obviously, it's true. But it suited John, and in some ways Chester before him—and frankly, it suited me, too—not to overplay it. There are some things you don't want to draw too much attention to, and the fact that you have a cash cow in London keeping you solvent in America is not something you necessarily trumpet around. It suited me because I had no ambitions to know what was happening in New Haven. I just didn't want them to interfere with what I was doing here." Given the fact that London is several thousand miles removed from New Haven, Nicoll said that he never felt that he had to develop a publishing list that might support the Yale curriculum in any way, nor did he feel that was one of his responsibilities. "As far as I was concerned, it was all publishing at a fairly serious level for academics and the interested general reader," he said.

As to exactly what his "ambitions" were, Nicoll said he had only one. "My ambition then, my ambition now, is to publish as many decent books as I can. There was an American whose name I can't recall who said the mission of a university press, the job of a university press, is to publish as many decent books as it can without going bankrupt. And that is roughly what I thought we should be trying to do. And there are all kinds of fundamental strategies you can pursue." Nicoll agreed that a good deal of his success undoubtedly came from the "confirmed business sense" he brought to the task. "My father was a businessman, and my late wife was a businesswoman, so I guess there is a fundamental issue there, which is not one we should probably be talking about, but one of the problems, I feel, with university presses is this cross-subsidy of books. This sort of thing is usually done in a very secretive, undiscussed, and what is probably an inappropriate sort of way. I'm not quite sure what the alternative would be, but usually it's sort of murky, how you decide which books you take on and which ones you don't."

Having said that there ought to be a "higher purpose" at play in the selection process, Nicoll acknowledged there is not "any adequate mechanism" to do it. "You'll go into an editorial meeting, you will say, this book is *really* good, but it's going to lose ten thousand pounds. Everybody else is going to tell you, 'We don't want to lose ten thousand pounds,' and there will be someone who says something else. So there is never any real honesty or transparency about this, and I'm not sure there can be. But we had lots of luck. We had the Mellon books that turned out to be no real strain on Yale's part, and, surprisingly, we managed to make some of them successful. Then we were in the right place with illustrated publishing, which I became quite interested in. And we were the pioneers among university presses in having a regular and significant list that we could sell to the trade every year. What I tried to do was to give the London office—the people there—the sense that this was their own show and that they could be proud of it."

Although the idea of a university press publishing large-format art books in a comprehensive manner by no means originated with Yale, the initiative reached new heights under Nicoll's leadership, not only for the beauty of the individual efforts, but for the unfailing excellence of their editorial content. Nobody, in other words, could mindfully call these efforts "coffee table books," a reference traditionally applied to oversized volumes filled with pretty pictures but having little in the way of trenchant commentary or original scholarship. Additional testimony to this are the relationships Yale has established over the past two decades with a number of outstanding museums to publish and distribute the catalogues of their major exhibitions, a good many of them blockbusters. Partnerships have been established with such institutions as the Metropolitan Museum of Art, the National Gallery of Art, the Art Institute of Chicago, and the National Gallery in London.

And Nicoll's sharp eye went well beyond illustrated books; one of his earliest triumphs was the publication in 1977 of *Caught in the Web of Words*, a biography of James A. H. Murray, for many years the principal editor and guiding spirit of the *Oxford English Dictionary;* the book was written by K. M. Elisabeth Murray, the great lexicographer's granddaughter. That was followed in 1978 by *Life in the English Country House: A Social and Architectural History*, an international success that enjoyed the dual distinction of winning several major awards for the architectural historian, Mark Girouard—the Duff

Cooper Memorial Prize and the W. H. Smith and Son Literary Award most prominent among them—while appearing
simultaneously on the London *Sunday Times* best-seller list.
Coming as it did in Kerr's final year at Yale, the Girouard success was "Chester's last hurrah," as John Ryden, his successor,
described it, and a telling example of Nicoll's expertise. In 1971,
while still an editor at Oxford, Nicoll had published an earlier
book by Girouard, *The Victorian Country House,* and though
a work of admirable scholarship, it was not the commercial
success its backers had expected. "It was a book that cried
out for illustrations, but it only had a handful of color plates,"
Ryden said. "John told me that he and Mark agreed that it
wasn't quite right, that there was a better way to do this, and
they wanted to try it again. So when John got to Yale, his idea
was to get the rights back from Oxford and reissue the same
book with lots of beautiful art. What they wanted to do was
completely integrate the illustrations in the text. Every page
had to be laid out precisely, and the type had to fit just so.
But in the midst of all that Mark got an assignment to give
the Slade Lectures at the National Gallery, so they decided to
develop a book from that instead, and that was called *Life in
the English Country House.* It was a huge success. It sold something like sixty thousand copies, and that happened just when
I was coming to Yale; the week before I started, paperback
rights were sold to Penguin for a hundred thousand pounds.
John started to build a great art list really from there."

Nicoll said the strategy he employed in producing art

books was decidedly hands-on for all the obvious reasons. "Initially, in the 1970s, we printed in the U.K., but they all went bankrupt. Then we started printing in Italy, and I spent a lot of my life in Milan, and later on in Prague, then in Hong Kong, and then in Singapore, overseeing each step of the process," he said. When asked what he was able to accomplish by tending to every detail himself, he ticked off a list of concerns. "You find mistakes that you can fix at the last minute, registration, color, or mistakes that are actually mistakes. With color printing, even black-and-white printing in those days, by being there, you can say, 'No, I don't like that. It's got to be better.' Another pair of eyes—a customer's eyes—sees things. The operator on the press simply wants to produce an acceptable job and go home. There may be problems of tracking, or running this picture next to that picture. Let's say this picture has a woman in a red dress, and this is a picture of snow. It's no surprise that snow gets a bit pink because it carries so much red ink to print the red dress. So someone has to strike a compromise. I knew that the only way I was going to get it right was to go there and sit on the press, to make sure it was right. You have to have someone who is interested and who asks, 'Why isn't this as good as that?' Or, 'Can we make this better?' They'll say, 'Yeah, we probably could, if we do this.' The Mark Girouard book was fairly easy. I saw all of that book being printed. As we grew, my colleagues who took over the design and production spent a lot of time with printers, too. It only stopped, I suppose, in the mid-nineties, because by then the printers finally had it right. They could do it most of the time. Initially, they got it wrong most of the time. But the standards were transformed between 1975 and 1990, too."

Looking back on more than thirty years as a publisher of books for an academic press, Nicoll said the task of choosing what to publish has subtleties that are unique unto themselves. "In trade publishing, you have to sense if people are going to be interested, and if they are, then it'll work. The judgment is still whether the book's any good, and it's usually a common man's judgment. 'Yes, it's literate, yes, it seems to touch the bases, yes, it's witty, yes, it's stylish, and so yes, we'll publish it.' But with an academic book, it's more difficult. You've got to know whether he really, or she really, has seen all the right archives, and read all the right articles, and sought all the appropriate documents. That's a pretty tricky go. What I always did, I used to use a very small circle of advisers who would tell me what they thought was good, and I relied on their judgment. I got what I thought was good advice."

Prizes, of course, are just one small measurement of success, but they are indicative of the esteem books have among their peers. Yale's virtual dominance of the Eric Mitchell Prize for the History of Art, an international competition inaugurated in 1976, can be reasonably compared to the run once enjoyed in Major League Baseball by the perennial champion New York Yankees, with Press authors winning sixteen top prizes through 2004, including honors for works about such artists and artistic figures as Georgio Vasari, Thomas Eakins, John Constable, Mark Rothko, and J. M. W. Turner and subjects as varied as Renaissance prints and eighteenth-century sculpture.

Nicoll was editor of the London division until 1985, when he was named managing director of the operation by John Ryden; he left in 2003 to assume direction of a trade press established by his wife, Frances Lincoln, who had died unexpectedly in 2001. He continues to publish illustrated books, along with a successful line of children's literature. "I had a fantastic time at Yale, and I loved it the whole time I was there," he told me. "What could be better than having a wealthy, benevolent, benign owner who lives several thousand miles away from you?" Nicoll's successor as managing director of the London division, Robert Baldock, has observed the unique nature of the operation since joining the Press as an acquisitions editor in 1985. "We've been able to make the money over the years," he told me, "because New Haven has to do a lot of things out of duty to its university. There are a lot of books they must publish that don't make money, so it doesn't actually make an operating profit, whereas we do. We don't have any endowment here; New Haven does have an endowment which provides them with a certain chunk of cash every year to subsidize, we don't. And so we have to operate like a normal business. We have to pay our salaries, and not make a loss, because if we make a loss, then we think that our masters in New Haven might say, 'Well, what is this operation for?'" By 2004, the London office was accounting for one hundred new Yale titles a year, 67 percent of them art books, the division's specialty, though hopes were expressed by Baldock at a Publications Committee meeting on April 24, 2004, "that this reliance will diminish" and that he would be acquiring new projects "geared toward greater sales potential in U.S. markets."

In his interview with me, Baldock touched on what he feels are the principal differences between New Haven and London. "The main thing is that we are three and a half thousand miles away from the university, so that liberates us to publish outside the box, while New Haven, to some extent, has to satisfy the academic community," he said. "It has to publish a certain number of monographs, specialist books, that these days you can't win with, whereas we are free of that, though to some extent we do publish very specialist books when one strikes us as an extraordinarily important book. But by and large, we go for books that have a bigger market." Baldock said that the London editors also are looking for books that tend to be more European in their scope, "and that maybe is the big difference" between the lists. "A lot of New Haven's books look at the U.S. experience in the world, and like every other American press, it publishes endless books on such subjects as the American Supreme Court, and things like that, which we can't sell here. Right now is an interesting time because just above the post-9/11 moment, Americans are looking at themselves and wondering why everybody dislikes them. So New Haven is producing more books about American concerns just at the time that the rest of the world is not buying them. I have great trouble telling my American colleagues that this is in fact the truth. America is big and rich and important and wealthy, and yes, it can do what it likes, and in terms of book publishing, it publishes lots of books about itself. But then they are mildly surprised that the rest of the world doesn't want to buy them."

What London can do for the mix, then, is to bring its own perspective. "We are not just an outpost of New Haven," Baldock stressed. "We are a separately constituted, self-conscious publisher of our own, with our own spirit. We are part of Yale and we take that seriously, and that is the reason we exist. But the books we do are different in their nature and their character from what New Haven does, and they fit if we slot them into the overall Yale list. Chester set up the London office quite brilliantly, it turns out, by making the imprint plausible to the rest of the world. There is nothing quite like having an imprint which is publishing books that literary editors here in the U.K. think are theirs. A lot of literary reviewers see us as a British press. They know, obviously, that we are owned by the U.S. and that we're all Yale employees, but they see us as a sort of little local press. Our books go out to them, and they see us as they do Granta or Faber or any of the others."

To illustrate the point, Baldock picked up a copy of *Thomas Cranmer: A Life*, by Diarmaid MacCulloch. "This came out in 1996, it got huge reviews, it won many trade prizes—

and it sold a lot of copies. That's exactly what we do best. We try to take an unlikely book, and make it work, because it's good. I think that is at the bottom of what we do." Baldock then turned to another book lying nearby, *A Little History of the World*, which Yale published in an English translation in 2005, some seventy years after it had appeared in Europe in eighteen other languages, and which had very quickly sold more than a hundred thousand copies for Yale. In this instance, the Press had taken what was ostensibly a book for children—the German art historian Ernst H. Gombrich, who died in 2001, had written the taut work to introduce young adults to the full sweep of Western civilization—and brought it to a new generation, in a new language. "It is a remarkable book, written in an amiable, conversational style, effortlessly explaining, without condescension, difficult matters like the achievements of Charlemagne, the monetary system of medieval Europe, and the ideas of the Enlightenment," Edward Rothstein wrote in the *New York Times*.

"We knew that Gombrich was the author of *The Story of Art*, and that basically he was a high-profile author," Baldock said. "Here you had a large subject, a little history of the world, so now you've got two of the components that you look for, and also the fact that he writes so beautifully, he's such a humane, sensitive man. So we knew it would do well, and we felt that people might say, 'Oh, what a nice little curiosity, what a sweet little book.'"

Because the London division is classified in the United

Kingdom as a charity—it is the American equivalent of a nonprofit entity—no corporate taxes are paid. "But then we don't make a whole lot of profit, because if we did, we'd just plow it all back into the books anyway, since we don't have any shareholders. Nobody's waiting to get money from us. If you make a better margin one year, then you can pay your staff better, you can pay bigger advances, you can hire that picture associate you've needed for years. But we aren't motivated by profit. We're motivated to pay our costs, and to pay authors promptly, and to pay our bills promptly—not to have a big balance in the bank."

In 1979, ten months after observing his sixty-fifth birthday, Chester Kerr stepped down as director of the Press and accepted an offer to become president of Ticknor and Fields, a newly revived imprint of Houghton Mifflin and once the publisher of such authors as Nathaniel Hawthorne, Henry Wadsworth Longfellow, Ralph Waldo Emerson, Harriet Beecher Stowe, and Mark Twain. Among the authors Kerr recruited for his lists were Calvin Trillin, John Mortimer, Olive Ann Burns, and his old Yale roommate, John Hersey. He died in 1999.

One of the hallmarks of the Kerr Report, published half a century earlier, was the no-nonsense observation it offered that in order to survive, scholarly publishers had to adopt some of the marketing and distribution methods employed by commercial publishers. In his 1949 *Publishers Weekly* interview, Kerr defended the practice of publishing "works of scholarship with commercial potential," calling it a way "of trying to place the university press in the mainstream of contributions to society. If—within the boundaries of scholarship always—we can make a contribution to culture, to politics, to the environment, then we shouldn't stand aside."

THREE

Enriching the Mix

HE RELATION BETWEEN AN ACA-
demic press and the institution whose
name it bears is unlike any other operation in the life of a university, and
the publishing initiative established by
George Parmly Day in 1908 on behalf
of his alma mater is a compelling case in point. For the first
half-century of its existence—a period embracing the full run
of the Day era—Yale University Press was a privately operated, not-for-profit entity that worked somewhat in tandem
with the administration but still had a great deal of separa-
tion from it, a degree of autonomy that had the potential to
create periodic points of conflict. When the Press became a
full department of the university in 1961, there was far greater
accountability, but given the fundamental nature of the enterprise—it is in the business of selling books, after all—there
was always the expectation that it make its own way.

"Universities expect their presses to be financially responsible," is the way deputy director and chief financial officer of the Press John Rollins put it during a wide-ranging
discussion we had one morning in his Temple Street office,
though the highly specialized nature of the product academic
publishers usually produce, he acknowledged, means that few
are in a position to cover their costs year after year. It is worth
noting that when we spoke in the summer of 2006, the Press
had reported $26 million in sales revenue for the fiscal year just
ended; in June 2007, the figure was $30.7 million—both very
much in the black. "A great many university presses require
operating subsidies from their universities, in fact most of
them do, and there are only a handful that actually manage
to break even," Rollins said. This particular observation came
in response to a question I put forth that asked, basically,
how it is that Yale is able to pay its own way so consistently.
Careful attention to the bottom line, it turns out, is just one
part of a coordinated approach to scholarly publishing that
is particularly suited to the vicissitudes of the twenty-first
century.

"We used to have standing orders with thousands of
libraries, and we don't have that anymore, so that's probably
the most dramatic change we have had to deal with," Rollins
said. Tina Weiner, associate director and publishing director
of the Press, was able to provide some detail on this unset-
tling phenomenon. "When I first came to the Press, the library market was robust and well funded, and because of our

standing orders, even our most scholarly titles could count on
a minimum level of sales that would be enviable today," she
said. "We are fortunate that our books have always enjoyed
a certain stature in the world of scholarly publishing. So you
had a stable income that was guaranteed, and even the most
monographic books—and so many of the books we do today
are equally as monographic now as they were then—would
just sell so much better. But with cutbacks in library funding,
the demise of the standing order—coupled with the demands
on budgets for electronic products—the library market for
most titles is severely curtailed. As a consequence, print runs
of academic books have plummeted and prices have escalated."
She cited several other trends the growth of the used book
market, especially for course adoption titles, and the wide-
spread practice of students and scholars alike photocopying
selections from books without obtaining the publishers' permission—as contributing to the decrease in average sales.

Most disturbing, perhaps, is the sharp decline in library
purchases of the scholarly monograph, a publishing concept
that has many definitions, few satisfactory. One definition
heard often is that a monograph is a book intended for an
academic audience, but a far more helpful guide, perhaps,
is a modification of the late Supreme Court justice Potter
Stewart's definition of pornography: "I know it when I see
it." However a monograph may or may not be defined, the
overriding reality is that fewer and fewer are being bought
by libraries. "There are books that we sell now, three to five

hundred copies, where we used to sell, easily, a thousand to fifteen hundred, without even trying that hard, because the library sale was so huge," Weiner said.

The most telling example she had to cite was a comparison of figures for the first book issued in the Papers of Benjamin Franklin series in 1959, and volume 37, released in 2003. "The first volume recorded sales of 8,100 copies, and it has gone downhill ever since," Weiner said, noting that after four years in print, volume 37 had recorded 700 copies sold. "You would think that the libraries that bought earlier volumes in such an important series would want complete sets, but obviously they don't, regardless of how distinguished that series is. What this tells you, in a pretty powerful way, is that the day of the standing order is over. It can't get more dramatic than that."

A detailed discussion of the seismic change in the way most academic libraries now do business is beyond the scope of this book, but certainly the most obvious reason for what has been happening over the past couple of decades stems partly from an increasing reliance on electronic sources of information in education and the continued marginalization of print materials. Books, it bears emphasizing, still matter a great deal, and any institution that covets respect and stature among its peers disdains acquiring them at its peril, as the University of California at Berkeley learned in the mid-1990s, when it began to scale down the level of its print acquisitions in favor of more electronic materials, a trend that prompted

the resignation in 1998 of its university librarian, Peter Lyman. "I think it is a horrendous and appalling mistake that
this university is not supporting the buying of books," Lyman
told me a few months before he announced his retirement.
"We are supposed to be the collection of record for the state
of California. If we don't collect something here, it probably
means that it does not exist in a research collection in this
state, perhaps in the West. And they've just abandoned that.
We are buying fewer and fewer books every year." Elsewhere
in our interview, Lyman offered this: "If the traditional marketplace for a product disappears, before long the product
itself will disappear. This is a legitimate concern I have over
the fate of the academic monograph." After slipping steadily
in its ranking among the one hundred and twenty members
of the Association of Research Libraries (ARL) over a three-
year period, Berkeley finally began budgeting more funds for
the purchase of books. At that point, criticism from within
the ranks—one tenured professor had wondered in a widely
quoted essay whether the university had "lost its soul"—began
to recede.

What this episode suggests rather convincingly is that
academic programs that are held in greatest esteem still maintain superior print collections and that one of the surest ways
for an emerging institution to gain respect is to create a great
library. At the top of the ARL rankings, Harvard University,
with more than 15.5 million volumes in its collections, continues to acquire books at a prodigious rate, reporting 429,344

"volumes added" in 2005; Yale, with 12 million volumes and ranked second only to Harvard in combined holdings, reported acquisitions of 302,604 volumes during the same period. As these robust figures suggest, neither program skimps on the purchase of scholarly research materials, be they print or electronic, and other participating institutions take care to maintain their places in this annual compilation too, even gloating a bit when they manage to move up in the ranks. Interestingly, the University of Toronto, with 10.3 million volumes, has placed third on the two most recent ARL lists, having moved up steadily from ninth in 1994, giving it the largest collection of any publicly supported institution in North America. Unlike so many state-supported universities in the United States that depend on governmental funding, Toronto has a "protected budget" dedicated to the purchase of print materials, one that is adjusted each year for inflation. "Our experience so far is that anything we have done electronically —and we have tried to stay at the leading edge in those fields—seems to result in people using more things in print," according to the chief librarian at the university, Carole Moore. For the vast majority of other institutions on the continent, however—and the American Library Association reports there are 117,467 libraries of all kinds in the United States, including 3,700 that are classified as academic—the annual purchase of books continues to decline.

A report prepared in 1996 by Brian L. Hawkins, at that time a vice president for academic planning and administration at Brown University, called "The Unsustainability of the Traditional Library and the Threat to Higher Education," correctly forecast that by the year 2001 academic libraries would be able to buy just 2 percent of the research materials they could afford two decades earlier, and that by the year 2026, "the acquisitions budgets of our finest libraries will have only 20 percent of the buying power they had forty-five years earlier." One solution suggested by Hawkins—and it has been embraced increasingly by cost-conscious libraries everywhere—was to commit increasing amounts of available funds to the purchase of computer equipment, software, and various online services, and less for printed books and journals. An immediate victim has been the practice of buying books on standing order from every manner of publisher, most ominously the scholarly presses that in many cases were established to serve that very market.

Another factor that has contributed mightily to reduced book purchases among academic libraries is the disappearance of government support. "Federal funding for higher education, which had been financing library acquisitions for years, was cut at the end of the Johnson administration," John Ryden told me. "When that was pulled out, there was a terrible downward spiral. All the publishers got hurt, first of all because they had inventory that they couldn't sell, then they cut their print runs, and then they raised their prices. At the same time libraries, especially college and university libraries, were beginning to spend even larger portions of their acquisition budgets on the sciences, and that meant more money on journal purchases, and more on technology. So today, it might be something like twenty-five cents out of every acquisition dollar in a university library that is going toward the buying of books."

A development of recent decades has been what for want of a better description can be called the consortium approach to book acquisition. With online catalogues of library holdings in place at every academic library in North America, institutions know what titles their colleagues own and thus are able to share books with one another through reciprocal lending agreements. "There has been an argument going on for some time among librarians that what is important today is not ownership but access," is the way Ray English, librarian of Oberlin College in Ohio—and with two million books to care for, he is custodian of the largest collection maintained by any undergraduate program in the United States—once explained the dynamic to me. "It is not a question of purchasing everything," he continued. "You need to carve out your own niche, which means you also need to draw on shared resources." One of the model arrangements of this kind operates in the Pioneer Valley of western Massachusetts at Amherst, Smith, Mount Holyoke, and Hampshire Colleges and the University of Massachusetts at Amherst. Known as the Five College Consortium, the program represents a kind of "collective" approach to librarianship that allows students from each of the schools to borrow books from the others. According to the most recent figures, nine million volumes

A. Bartlett Giamatti, president of Yale University, 1978–1986, and John G. Ryden, director of Yale University Press, 1979–2002, celebrate the Press's seventy-fifth anniversary in 1983 *(Photo: Yale University Office of Public Affairs)*

Benno C. Schmidt, Jr., president of Yale University, 1986–1992, toasts Edward P. Evans, Class of 1964, at a reception announcing the alumnus's $1.25 million gift to Yale University Press

The Evans Wing, completed in 1993 *(Engraving: Jon DePol)*

302 Temple Street, the Press's seventh and current home *(Engraving: Jon DePol)*

Joanna Rose, Yale University Press supporter, at the publication
party for *The Encyclopedia of New York City* in 1995

From left: John Rollins, Tina Weiner, Meryl Lanning, Charles Grench, Paul Royster, and
John Ryden on the occasion of Tina Weiner's twenty-fifth anniversary at the Press in 1996

Jaroslav Pelikan *(Photo: John Earle)*

From left: Jonathan Brent, executive editor of the Press, with William F. Buckley, Jr., an early supporter of the Annals of Communism series, and Senator Daniel Patrick Moynihan at the Yale Club NYC in 2001

David Bromwich, Sterling Professor of English, Yale University, and chairman, Yale University Press Publications Committee, with Peter Workman, chairman, Yale University Press Board of Governors *(Photo: Harold Shapiro)*

The George Parmly Day Library, 302 Temple Street

From left: John Donatich, Theodore Margellos, Iliodora Margellos, Class of 2006, Cecile Margellos, Richard Levin, president of Yale University, and his wife, Jane Levin, 2007 *(Photo: Michael Marsland)*

are readily available throughout the network, with a courier system in place that promises delivery within twenty-four hours of each request. What this means is that monographic imprints need no longer be acquired by every institution in the consortium. In most cases, one copy is deemed sufficient. While such streamlining allows college and university libraries to groom their holdings and cut their costs, university presses have had to consider creative ways to market their new releases elsewhere in order to survive.

At Yale, the Press has always been expected to cover its operating costs, regardless of the changes that have taken place in the marketplace. Since becoming a formal department of the university in 1961, the Press has been eligible to receive a portion of the general endowment, which in 2007 was reported at $22.5 billion, an all-time high for Yale and second only to Harvard, which reported $34.9 billion for the same period. "In all fairness, that's a considerable advantage that the larger presses have," Rollins acknowledged. "Not all of our colleagues have endowments, but Princeton, Harvard, and Yale, for example, do, and it helps each of us a great deal. The way the Yale endowment works is that it's all centrally invested and managed, and each unit within the university has shares. It's almost like a mutual fund. What we have is so many shares in the university's endowment." The stipend fluctuates from year to year as the size of the endowment fluctuates. "That, basically, is seed money that we use as working capital to invest in our future. That money is there largely to invest in books. That's the difference, because our financial goal is to break even on the bottom line—in the best of times at the operating line. In some years we manage to do that, some years we don't. If we break even at the operating line, then our endowment income is money that we can use to plow back into the program to do special things, to do new things, to do different things." In fiscal year 2007, the Press published 253 hardcover titles and 85 paperbacks.

Frank M. Turner, John Hay Whitney Professor of History and director of the Beinecke Rare Book and Manuscript Library at Yale, has witnessed Press operations from a variety of vantage points during the past four decades. A member of the faculty since 1970, Turner was university provost from 1988 to 1992, a position that made him the chief academic officer during that period and a key figure in the administration. He also has served on the Publications Committee of the Press and has helped determine many of the lists that have been ushered into print. Among his own scholarly works, five have been published with Yale, including *John Henry Newman: The Challenge to Evangelical Religion* (2002), esteemed by some colleagues as his magnum opus, and *Between Science and Religion: The Reaction to Scientific Naturalism in Late Victorian England* (1974), a revision of his doctoral dissertation; so he has thoughts on that particular dynamic as well.

Reflecting on the years he spent as provost, Turner told me that it mattered a great deal to his colleagues in the administration that the Press pay its own way. "We were concerned that it operate in the black because we really didn't have the money to subsidize it," he said, noting that the remarkable endowment Yale now enjoys is a consequence only of the past decade. One of the first observations Turner had to offer when we spoke one hot summer morning in his office at the Beinecke—the university's chief repository of rare books and manuscripts and one of the outstanding treasure houses of knowledge maintained in the world—was that university presses, in general, "tend to operate by courtesy," a phrase that was new to me, certainly in this context, and I asked him to explain. "By that," he replied, "I mean they exist *within* universities, but that does not mean that universities, as a rule, are necessarily going to subsidize them. They may help them get off the ground, or they may give them bridge money if there's a difficult period, but they don't usually subsidize them. So presses have to publish what faculties and scholars want, but they also have to publish things that are going to allow those other publications to take place."

Turner used another phrase—"creative tension"—to describe the responsibility of a university to work with scholars whose efforts might otherwise go unpublished. "The expectation that a certain number of books would always be purchased by university libraries no longer applies, and it has had an impact on the way business is conducted," he said. "The whole system used to depend upon a certain kind of financing of guaranteed sales. That's no longer the case, and that's why in order to produce some of these other books that I feel ought to be published, I have no trouble with the Press publishing other books that do sell."

Because of all this, Turner continued, a university press has to have a "clear view" of what it is trying to accomplish. "University presses at the moment are all facing great challenges. Yale's doing very well, but it has very sprightly conversations in-house and with the Publications Committee and elsewhere about what it should be publishing. When I was starting in the profession back in the early 1970s, it was assumed that if you had written a good dissertation—not any dissertation, but if you had written a good dissertation—you would find a publisher in a major university press. Your book in those days would probably sell maybe fifteen hundred, two thousand copies. Well, that just isn't the case anymore. My own sense is that in the last twenty-five years, university presses have been drawn more fully into the larger world of publication, rather than just being out there on their own. At Yale, you have the Chester Kerr era to reflect on, and you undoubtedly have heard a lot about that, but I think the person who is really responsible for the Press as it is today, and for the commercial success it enjoys, as you just defined it, as probably the most successful university press in the country, is John Ryden."

Ryden, Turner said, "was as different from Chester Kerr as can be. I didn't know Chester all that well, but Chester was mercurial and he sought to be—and he was—a kind of larger-than-life figure. Ryden just got the work done. He liked talented people, and he was willing to have talented people working for him who didn't always get along with each other. My sense is that if he had an editor who was good, he would give that editor a lot of leash and allow for a lot of entrepreneurial work. And he was there long enough to create a culture and to put into place business plans that actually are coming to fruition today." Of overriding importance, Turner added, is that Ryden "didn't think the Press was all about him."

Like Kerr, Ryden came to the Press as a book professional who had been trained in the publishing industry, but unlike Kerr, he was not a member of the Yale old boys' club. Ryden's alma mater is Harvard, Class of 1961, and when he came to interview for the director's position in 1979, he was employed as editor-in-chief and associate director of the University of Chicago Press. Before that he was executive editor at Harper and Row; he began his career in publishing in the sales department at McGraw-Hill after serving a tour of duty as a naval intelligence officer.

Ryden told me that one of his earliest realizations on assuming the Yale directorship was that the old models were no longer working. "The biggest challenge I think that all university presses have faced from the mid-1970s on is how to make a go of it, because selling the books that they were publishing wasn't paying the costs, and some presses never recovered from that." Indeed, he added, a few operations almost went out of business. "A lot of others scaled down, and they still couldn't handle it. At Yale, it was certainly my biggest challenge, not just the editions of Franklin and so on—and Yale published fifteen or twenty of these series books; there were many huge projects we were committed to—but any kind of standard monograph. I'm thinking here of the revised dissertation that gets published, or a tenure book, for instance. We wanted to keep doing that, but it wasn't working financially, so ways had to be found to bring in enough income; something else had to be done."

That "something else," he realized, was to develop a strategy in which the entire list would pay for itself, and the way to achieve that, he determined, was to "enrich the mix of books" with titles that had a wider appeal, an approach to publishing employed successfully in the commercial sector and one he thought could be applied at Yale. Ryden mentioned his former employer, Harper and Row, which is now HarperCollins, as one trade house that pursues such a policy, but there are others, Alfred A. Knopf in the Random House/Bertelsmann group, Farrar, Straus and Giroux (within Holtzbrinck), and W. W. Norton (which has both college and trade divisions), for instance, that are just as successful with it. In his London interview with me, John Nicoll had another phrase for the concept—he called it the "cross-subsidy of books"—which means, basically, that profits earned from titles that make money are used to underwrite monographic works that typically do not. "I came to Yale from the University of Chicago Press, which has a strong journals program, and I toyed for a while with the idea of doing something with journals, but it quickly became clear to me it wasn't possible to do that at Yale, where the strengths are in the humanities," Ryden said. "So it was then that I decided that what I wanted to do was enrich the mix of books, and we did that in several ways. One of them was to get the very same scholars who wrote monographs to write bigger books on broader subjects." The first place Ryden decided to look was in his own backyard. "Whether it was Peter Gay or C. Vann Woodward or Ed Morgan, there have always been people of great stature at Yale who can go anywhere to publish, and very often they do exactly that. So one of the things I did when I arrived in New Haven was try to recapture some of these people for our list."

Ryden's first notable success in this pursuit, the Yale historian of religion Jaroslav Pelikan, turned out to be an inspiration. At the time of his death in 2006 at eighty-two, Pelikan had written forty well-received books, his best-known effort a five-volume work published during the 1970s by the University of Chicago Press, *The Christian Tradition: A History of the Development of Doctrine*. Ryden said he first became acquainted with Pelikan while at Harper and Row, where Pelikan served briefly as academic adviser and which brought out several of his books in paperback editions. "I was the history editor there for a while, and I got to know him pretty well. This happened at a time when trade publishing was approaching Jary in a big way, and he very easily could have gone to other places," Ryden said. "He had talked to Harper about a few things, but they never came to pass, and then he had written a proposal for *Reader's Digest* about a big project that excited him, but they backed out. They paid him, as I recall, twenty-five thousand dollars just to write the proposal, and then decided it was too complicated for them. They just couldn't get a handle on what he had in mind, apparently. So when I came to Yale, I said, 'We can publish you in a way that I think Harper wanted to, and the way *Reader's Digest* I'm sure wanted to, and we can give you a broader audience.' I assured him that we would do a real proper job in publishing these serious books he had in mind."

What carried the day for Ryden was his suggestion that Pelikan deliver a series of public lectures in New Haven on a project that he had been tinkering with for years—the same project, in fact, that he had sketched out for *Reader's Digest*— and that he adapt the oral presentations for the text of a book that Yale would then publish. The result was *Jesus through the Centuries: His Place in the History of Culture,* which appeared in 1985. Once the book was published, and as glowing reviews began to appear on both sides of the Atlantic, it was obvious that Ryden had hit a home run. Pelikan later told the *New York Times* that it was those lectures, each one given twice a week at the Yale Law School Auditorium over a five-month period (the five-hundred-seat hall was too small to accommodate the demand) that gave him "the opportunity to write the book I always wanted to write." *Jesus through the Centuries* went on to sell more than forty thousand copies in hardcover, a heady figure for a work that examined two thousand years of quotations, observations, and interpretations of Jesus, featuring relevant excerpts from the Gospels to Dante, from Thomas Jefferson to Albert Schweitzer. "I was off to a running start," Ryden said. "Then we sold the paperback rights to Harper for a hundred thousand dollars. Later, we published an illustrated edition, and a while after that Jary wrote *The Illustrated Mary*, a companion volume." Throughout his years at Yale, Pelikan was a great champion of the Press and its activities, serving variously as chairman of the Publications Committee and as vice president of its Board of Governors. In an address he gave in 1992 to the charter meeting of the Friends of Yale University Press, a fundraising group, titled "The University's Secret Weapon," Pelikan had this to say about the works he felt a scholarly press ought to be publishing:

> Whereas we as the Yale University faculty must continue to base decisions of appointment and tenure on the solidity of scholarship as evidence in the quality of research and teaching, we as Yale University Press are free to take somewhat greater risks, by publishing books also by some scholars whose audacity of speculation seems even greater than the quality of their research. The acceptable limits for such risks are a matter of constant concern and continuing review. If I were forced to do so, I could (though I won't) identify Yale University Press authors and titles in recent years that have, in my judgment, gone beyond those limits—as well as others that at the time appeared to be doing so but that seem to have been vindicated in their speculations. That is precisely

the sort of risk that a press can take even when a tenure committee can't.

For Ryden, giving Pelikan the widest audience possible for his writing and suggesting follow-up projects "were all very commercial things to do," and heralded a new direction for the Press. "After that we began to publish in earnest some textbooks, building on a pre-existing strength, which did very well, too. For the next fifteen years those textbooks brought in on average a million dollars a year." In 1994, one text alone, *French in Action*, by Pierre J. Capretz, Béatrice Abetti, Marie-Odile Germain, and Laurence Wylie, recorded $1.4 million in sales, according to an annual report given that year to the Board of Governors. "And the art and art history list that was largely published out of our London office continued to grow and get very strong too," Ryden said. "So we were doing three things that university presses traditionally didn't do—trade books, textbooks, and art books—and that basically is how we made a go of it. That was our bread and butter. We were the pioneers among American university presses to have a regular and significant list that we could sell to the trade every year, and we did it quite successfully."

Because he approached the Pelikan book with the mindset of a trade publisher, Ryden had an expectation of commercial success. Just as rewarding, he added, were books that "took off" entirely of their own account. One was a book edited by the eminent Yale historian C. Vann Woodward of a nineteenth-century journal written by Mary Chesnut, the wife of a high-ranking Confederate official, and titled *Mary Chesnut's Civil War,* which became a best seller when issued in 1981. Woodward was a well-known and highly respected historian, so although the commercial success of Chesnut's journal may have been a pleasant surprise, the critical approbation the book received, including a Pulitzer Prize in 1982, was by no means unpredictable. Far more startling, to Ryden's mind—he cited it as his favorite example—was the response to a book he acquired in 1998 with very little expectation for sales, merely a case of taking on a book he and his colleagues felt justified publication by a university press. "We bought the American rights from I. B. Tauris, a small London publisher that specializes in books on the Middle East, and it was called *Taliban: Militant Islam, Oil and Fundamentalism in Central Asia.* It was published in a hardcover edition in 2000, and by our standards sold quite nicely, about four thousand copies. The following summer, we brought out a paperback edition, and it began to sell at the same rate. Then, when September 11, 2001, came along, there was not another book out there where people could find out who the Taliban were. I remember when the book was first proposed, I said something like, 'Who's the Taliban?' I didn't know who they were myself. And in the next month and a half we sold in the neighborhood of three hundred thousand copies. It hit number one on the *New York Times* paperback list one week, and stayed on the list for several months after that. It surely had its moment. And the fellow who wrote it, Ahmed Rashid, a Pakistani, had his moment as well; he was interviewed on national television by Peter Jennings, Charlie Rose, Larry King, and a few others." That is a case, Ryden said, "of a book that was published with no expectations; it just told a story, that's all," and when world events made the subject it discussed a matter of consuming public interest, sales soared. Ryden cited another example that, though much less dramatic, was similar in the circumstances of its sudden relevance and sales potential. "In 1978, the Press published the *English-Khmer Dictionary*, which was essentially a field guide to basic words and phrases in the Khmer language. When refugees started coming into the United States from Cambodia during the Pol Pot years, it was the only book of its kind; the Press sold about thirty thousand copies of that, and would have been perfectly satisfied with five hundred."

A project proposed in 1992 by John Nicoll in the London office to take over a distinguished series of books published in the United Kingdom by the trade publisher Penguin known as the Pelican History of Art met with a degree of skepticism in New Haven but received the enthusiastic support of Ryden. Initiated in 1953 by Allen Lane, the founder of Penguin, and edited by the German-born architect and art historian Nikolaus Pevsner, the series of illustrated hardcover art histories and surveys had secured a devoted following in its time, but had become unprofitable under its more recent ownership, Pearson, Ltd. Nicoll had proposed "adopting" the series, as Ryden described it, including its backlist, with the idea of producing updated, streamlined editions and offering them as inexpensive paperbacks. At the February 24, 1992, meeting of the Publications Committee, Ryden countered one member's view that the idea was not an appropriate venture for the Press to consider—the precise words used were that it was "not right"—by saying he thought it was a "very special opportunity" to "acquire and distribute the existing volumes and remaining contracted books" in the series while introducing new efforts that would "stand on the shoulders" of their predecessors. "How will this be done?" Ryden asked: "We will consult with the scholarly community. Mr. Nicoll will edit the series, which will have its own editorial board." The critical response to the spruced-up books was overwhelmingly positive. In a holiday roundup of art books published by the *New York Times* in 1995, John Russell called it "a happy day when the Yale University Press took over the Pelican History of Art." By the fall of 2007, sixty-six titles in the series were on the backlist. Following hard on that success, the Press took over another notable series, the Pevsner Architectural Guides to the Buildings of England, Ireland, Scotland, and Wales.

Any examination of the minutes of Publications Committee and Finance Committee meetings over the past three decades turns up periodic reference to the goal of achieving balance in the list. At a December 7, 1995, meeting of the Board of Governors, Jonathan Spence asked whether "it was still the Press's intention to expand the list as had been previously discussed." Ryden answered that the list had already expanded and that "we are publishing more titles than ever before"—at that time 185 new hardcover titles on the list, compared to 170 a year earlier and 150 the year before that. Spence then wondered what "the difference is between the trade list and the Press's other titles. Are sharper distinctions being drawn?" Tina Weiner said that as the sale of scholarly monographs continued to decline, "it has become increasingly important to have titles with broader appeal that can be counted on to sell to wider audiences through general retail outlets." That said, however, "we are doing more monographs than ever before," Ryden added.

At a meeting on October 2, 2001, a good deal of the talk was about the astounding sales of Ahmed Rashid's *Taliban,* with 150,000 copies sold in less than a month of the terrorist attacks on the World Trade Center in New York and the Pentagon in Washington. There were some other surprising sales figures to share as well. Weiner reported that *Five Days in London,* by John Lukacs, a book that had been in print for two years, had sold 60,000 copies in cloth and 25,000 copies in paper in a matter of weeks, and the reason she gave for that astounding development was the ringing endorsement the book had received from New York mayor Rudy Giuliani in the immediate aftermath of 9/11. In numerous national interviews he gave at the time, Giuliani said Lukacs's narrative of how Winston Churchill had convinced his cabinet in

May 1940 that Britain should fight alone against Germany if necessary, had been an "inspiration" to him. One of Giuliani's favorite passages from the book was this gem. "An appeaser," the prime minister had told his colleagues, "is one who feeds a crocodile hoping it will eat him last."

Sales of *Taliban* continued well into 2002, with Ryden making special note of its remarkable success as the fiscal year was ending. "This year we had *Taliban*," he told the Board of Governors on June 14, "next year we won't. And because of that we are projecting sales to decline by roughly $1 million." Later in the meeting, Weiner expressed high hopes for several titles on the forthcoming list, words that would prove prophetic, most tellingly her enthusiasm for Edmund Morgan's *Benjamin Franklin*, which before long would sell 120,000 copies in hardcover. She also took optimistic note of the prospects for *Why Terrorism Works: Understanding the Threat, Responding to the Challenge*, a timely commentary on current affairs by the celebrity lawyer Alan Dershowitz—that book would sell more than 30,000 copies—and *Churchill: Visionary, Statesman, Historian*, a new work by John Lukacs being published hard on the heels of the celebrity generated by his *Five Days in London*. Additionally, there were gratifying numbers to report from a recent release that had already sold 7,300 copies in hardcover, *Lichens of North America*, by Irwin M. Brodo, Sylvia Duran Sharnoff, and Stephen Sharnoff, accounting for three hundred thousand dollars in gross revenue. Equally as satisfying was that the book on lichens had just been named winner of the R. R. Hawkins Award for outstanding scholarly or reference work of 2001, a prize presented annually by the Association of American Publishers.

Frank Turner's observation that Ryden was the kind of director who encouraged editors to be creative was rewarded with a number of successes. One editor who was already working at the Press when Ryden arrived in New Haven in 1979, Edward Tripp, earned a reputation as a person who was constantly coming up with wonderful ideas for new projects. "Ed was a very sweet guy," Turner recalled. "When I published my first book with Yale in 1974, he had already been with the Press for a couple of years. He impressed me as a very creative kind of person who could just generate interesting projects. He'd say things like, 'Why don't we try this, why don't we try that?' You have to understand that Yale works through friendships, with editors who cultivate people and who are not shy about asking, 'What's going on in your life? Maybe we need a series here.' These editors make it a point to work with authors and stay in touch. So when finally an author has a manuscript, that author is likely to say, 'You know, I'm going to bring it to Yale.'"

Tripp spent twenty years working as a social worker in New York City and as a professional violinist before entering publishing in 1959 to head up the reference department at T. Y. Crowell, a house that later became an imprint of Harper-Collins. He joined the Press in July 1971 and was named editor-in-chief in 1973, a position he held until his retirement in 1990. When Tripp died nine years later at seventy-nine, Ryden called him "the most imaginative and wide-ranging editor that I worked with" at Yale. An idea Tripp came up with in 1982 for a first-of-its-kind *Encyclopedia of New York City* illustrates perfectly Ryden's goal of seeking out impeccably researched books with solid commercial potential, as well as Turner's description of a person who was always thinking of exciting publishing avenues to explore. The Columbia University historian Tripp approached to be general editor of the project, Kenneth T. Jackson, remembered being called one day by a total stranger and presented with a proposal to produce a one-volume compendium of information, essays, and details that were fascinating, curious, and arcane about the history, culture, landmarks, neighborhoods, personalities, idioms, and lore of America's largest and most vibrant metropolis. Fascinated by the suggestion, and seduced by the opportunity he was being offered "to put more than 370 years of New York City history between two covers," Jackson signed on immediately.

Funding for the project was raised by the Press in collaboration with the New-York Historical Society, which arranged contributions from private donors, with the largest individual grant, $350,000, coming from the Gladys and Roland Harriman Foundation. Ultimately, close to $1 million would be raised to support the ambitious undertaking. Initial plans called for a book of about 840,000 words, but "the project just grew and grew," according to Fred Kameny, the Yale editor who took over supervision of the project after Tripp retired. By the time the encyclopedia was released in 1995, the word count had doubled. One of Kenneth Jackson's responsibilities had been to recruit scores of authorities to write the 4,288 entries, some 680 people in all. "No one with even a passing interest in New York will be able to live without it," enthused the *New York Times*. Despite its sixty-five-dollar price tag at publication—it now retails at seventy-five dollars—the seven-and-a-half-pound book sold briskly, going through five printings through 2007, recording sales of 70,000 copies in hardcover. Other one-volume Yale encyclopedias have followed, including *The New Encyclopedia of the American West* (1998), winner of the Western Heritage Award sponsored by the Cowboy Hall of Fame and edited by Howard R. Lamar, Sterling Professor Emeritus of History at Yale and president of the university from 1992 to 1993; the Howard R. Lamar Center for the Study of Frontiers and Borders at Yale was named in his honor in 2000. Other similar compendia of note: *Encyclopedia of Underwater and Maritime Archaeology* (1998), edited by James P. Delgado and published in association with the British Museum Press; *The Holocaust Encyclopedia* (2001), edited by Walter Laqueur, cochairman of the International Research Council of the Center for Strategic and International Studies, and undertaken with the assistance of a major grant from the Hollywood director Steven Spielberg; *The Encyclopedia of Ireland* (2003), edited by Brian Lalor; and *The Encyclopedia of New England* (2005), edited by Burt Feintuch and David

H. Watters, which through the fall of 2007 had sold more than 10,000 copies.

Though *The Encyclopedia of New York City* was Tripp's splashiest project, he shepherded many others along to publication, as a number of grateful authors have acknowledged in their books. In the preface to *Armed Martial Arts of Japan: Swordsmanship and Archery* (1998), for example, G. Cameron Hurst III, a professor of history and director of the Center for East Asian Studies at the University of Pennsylvania, wrote this: "The project had its genesis when Edward Tripp, editor at Yale University Press, contacted me about it, far longer ago than I now choose to recall. But I still remember the scene vividly. It was during the summer, and I was home eating lunch when Mr. Tripp called to say that Yale University Press was interested in a book on the martial arts. Would I be interested in writing it? I was taken aback, and my immediate reaction was to look for Allen Funt lurking behind the couch with camera in hand. 'Am I on Candid Camera?'"

During his thirteen years at Yale, Tripp acquired about two hundred books for the Press, and in a stunning variety of subjects. Among the titles he guided into print: *The Bonds of Womanhood: "Woman's Sphere" in New England, 1780–1835,* by Nancy F. Cott; *A Handbook of Clinical Dietetics,* by the American Dietetic Association; *Vampires, Burial, and Death: Folklore and Reality,* by Paul Barber; *The Chronicle of the Łódź Ghetto, 1941–1944,* by Lucjan Dobroszycki; *The Composer's Advocate,* by Erich Leinsdorf; *Paganism in the Roman Empire,* by Ramsay

MacMullen; *A Handbook of Russian Literature,* edited by Victor Terras; *Cosmos, Earth, and Man: A Short History of the Universe,* by Preston Cloud; and *The Origins of Sex: Three Billion Years of Genetic Recombination,* by Lynn Margulis. At the March 26, 1990, meeting of the Publications Committee, Jaroslav Pelikan proposed a toast to Tripp on the eve of his retirement. "If you want a monument, just look about you," he said, paraphrasing a quotation once used to describe the four-decade-long effort of Sir Christopher Wren to rebuild Saint Paul's Cathedral in London. During Tripp's years at the Press, Pelikan continued, "the list has grown in size, but it has also borne the marks of his light touch (as in his famous covering letters) and of his interest in unusual topics (as, for example, vampires). And so I would rewrite Milton's "L'Allegro": 'Come and Trippe it as ye grow, With a light fantastic glow.'"

It is tempting, of course, to list all the other notable books published by the Press during these fruitful years, a daunting exercise if ever there was one, though a few certainly do cry out for individual mention: *The Madwoman in the Attic: The Woman Writer and the Nineteenth-Century Literary Imagination* (1979), by Sandra M. Gilbert and Susan Gubar; *Hannah Arendt: For Love of the World* (1982), by Elisabeth Young-Bruehl; *Velázquez: Painter and Courtier* (1986), by Jonathan Brown; *Impressionism: Art, Leisure, and Parisian Society* (1988), by Robert L. Herbert; *Giovanni Bellini* (1989), by Rona Goffen; *America's Rome* (1990), by William L. Vance; *Sexual Personae: Art and Decadence from Nefertiti to Emily Dickinson* (1990), by Camille

Paglia; *Holocaust Testimonies: The Ruins of Memory* (1991), by Lawrence L. Langer; *The Stripping of the Altars: Traditional Religion in England, c. 1400–c. 1580* (1992), by Eamon Duffy; *Opera in America: A Cultural History* (1993), by John Dizikes; *William Tyndale: A Biography* (1994), by David Daniell; and *The Spanish Inquisition: A Historical Revision* (1998), by Henry Kamen. A sampling, to be sure, but remarkable books that shared the distinction of making an impact while reaching appreciative readerships.

In 1991, Ryden hired Jonathan Brent, a forty-year-old scholar with a doctorate in English from the University of Chicago who had made a name for himself in the 1980s as director of Northwestern University Press, at that time a moribund publishing program that he had restored to respectability. Brent studied Russian literature as a Columbia undergraduate and has translated a number of works into English, including poems by the Russian-born poet Joseph Brodsky and the *Confession of Isaac Babel* for his book *Inside the Stalin Archives* (2008). With his wife, Frances Padorr Brent, a poet and professional translator, Brent in 1984 founded *Formations,* a literary quarterly specializing in the works of Eastern European writers, including a number of dissidents active during the final years of the Soviet Union. Ryden said Brent impressed him immediately as an "imaginative and extremely aggressive editor" who wasted little time in making "a huge difference" in the direction the Press would take into the twenty-first century. In 1997, Brent would be named editorial director, and in

2001 associate director, all the while coming up with ideas for new projects, but none more spectacular than an opportunity that came his way within weeks of his hiring in 1991.

Barely a month into the job, Brent attended a conference in Prague at the invitation of George Soros, the Hungarian-born financial speculator who had been a patron of *Formations* and who continues to be an active supporter of various philanthropic causes around the world. In Prague, Soros and Brent heard a scholar talk about research being done in Czech archives. "I stopped him cold," Brent told me. "I said, 'You mean the former Communist government of Czechoslovakia? You are looking at those archives?' He said that was correct. I turned to Soros and said, 'There's got to be stuff in those archives worth publishing, worth knowing. We have to start a series, and we'll call it something like the Documents of Totalitarianism.' I was excited because I knew this literature— I wasn't a historian, but I knew this literature." A few inquiries among contacts in Eastern Europe further persuaded Brent that access to materials in the secret files of the former Soviet Union was a distinct possibility as well, and he moved quickly on his hunch. "I went to John Ryden in October 1991," Brent said, "and he told me one thing, 'Go to Moscow. Let's see what you come up with.' I don't know of another press director in America at that time who wouldn't have sat down right away with a calculator and said, 'Okay, how much is this going to cost? Where is the money going to come from? How many books can we possibly sell? What do you have planned?' That

was a great relief to me, because I couldn't possibly have answered any of that." To get him started, George Soros wrote
out a check for thirty-six thousand dollars. "It wasn't a lot of
money," Brent said, "but it gave me what I needed to get to
Moscow in January of 1992 and determine what was there.
That money enabled me to meet with the heads of the archives
and to make the deal; it also enabled me to have some sense
that I could get more money and make this thing work. It was
a classic case of one thing leading to another."

After several months of prolonged negotiations, Brent
hammered out an understanding whereby the Press agreed to
publish a series of scholarly works that would use documents
from Soviet archives as primary sources, a circumstance that
would have been unthinkable just a year earlier. He agreed
to reproduce the documents both in Russian and in English
translation and to publish them in volumes containing commentary from American and Russian scholars. Not everything
was open to scrutiny, however—some archivists placed restrictions on their material, other files remained off-limits—yet
an enormous amount of information was made available. "I
had to recruit writers, I had to hire scholars and researchers,
I developed an editorial committee," Brent said. "There were
people who told me the project was impossible, there were
just too many files to wade through. I said, 'We have research
teams who will go in there, find the material, and develop
it all into specific projects.' When I got started on this, all I
knew was that there is a lot of secret material in those files,

and it has to be good. That's all I knew. I didn't even know what the Comintern was when I got over there. All of my understanding of Soviet history came through Isaak Babel and Anna Ahkmatova, I had no idea who Vishinsky was, I knew of Molotov only because of the cocktail. But this is what I did know: I knew that when I was a kid I hid under desks in the basement of my school because of the Soviet Union. When Sputnik went up, there was panic in my school. I remember the army-McCarthy hearings, I remember my parents arguing about Alger Hiss. So I knew that this was material of world importance. I knew this history had shaped who we are. And I knew that it wasn't going to go away. So, I began to learn. Boy, I learned."

The Iron Curtain had been down barely four years before the first release in what became known as the Annals of Communism series appeared in 1995; titled *The Secret World of American Communism*, the book was written jointly by Harvey Klehr, a professor of politics and history at Emory University; John Earl Haynes, a specialist in twentieth-century political history in the Manuscript Division of the Library of Congress; and Fridrikh Igorevich Firsov, the former head of the Comintern Archive at the Russian Center for the Preservation and Study of Documents of Recent History. Central to their narrative were ninety-two documents from the Comintern archives that offered persuasive evidence that the Communist Party of the United States had been deeply involved in espionage against the United States during the 1950s. The papers also seemed to validate the claim by Whittaker Chambers, the man who originally accused Alger Hiss of spying against the United States, that an elaborate network of Soviet agents was working in Washington during the 1930s. Other disclosures indicated that the late American billionaire Armand Hammer had laundered money for the Soviets and that Edmund Stevens, a prominent Moscow-based reporter, was on the Soviet payroll.

By 2008, twenty titles had been published in the series, with more in various stages of preparation. Others published thus far have included *The History of the Gulag: From Collectivization to the Great Terror* (2004), by Oleg V. Khlevniuk, for which Brent hired a dozen Russian researchers to comb through the Comintern archives, and *The Unknown Lenin: From the Secret Archive* (1999), by the Harvard historian Richard Pipes and Yuri A. Buranov. One of the most controversial volumes to appear has been *Spain Betrayed: The Soviet Union in the Spanish Civil War* (2001), by Ronald Radosh, Mary R. Habeck, and G. N. Sevostianov, which documented extensive Soviet support of the Republican forces during the Spanish Civil War. "Everything that was ever suspected about the Comintern line in Spain turns out to have been true," Christopher Hitchens wrote in the *Wilson Quarterly*. "If Spain were Vietnam," Sam Tanenhaus wrote in *Vanity Fair*, "these would be its Pentagon Papers." In the spring of 2007, the Press and the Hoover Institution at Stanford University announced they were finalizing an arrangement to digitize and publish material from Stalin's personal archive, including correspondence about the purges of the 1930s and the immediate postwar period. "It's like the Dead Sea Scrolls for the Stalin period," Brent told one interviewer, adding his view that the material will provide "a sense of Stalin the individual, his psychology, his growth as a leader."

Since its release more than a decade ago, *The Secret World of American Communism* has sold the most copies of all in the series, some sixteen thousand copies in hardcover, another three thousand in paper, many of them to libraries. While these are respectable numbers, they are hardly sufficient to support such an ambitious undertaking that has involved the work of so many people. And given the nature of such highly charged material, with people who continue to be seriously divided politically on these matters, financial backing has not been easy to secure. "I had the green light to go ahead with the project, but I had to do it entirely with outside money," Brent made clear to me. "I went to some of the big foundations, like Ford and MacArthur, and they turned us down flat. I have had to raise a huge amount of money—over a million dollars so far—and I'm in the process of raising more now."

But there were fortuitous moments for which Brent said he remains profoundly grateful all the same. Not long after the publication of *The Secret World of American Communism,* he received a letter of congratulations from Daniel Patrick Moynihan, a former U.S. ambassador to India and the United Nations who at that time was the senior senator from New

York. Moynihan also was chairman of the bipartisan Commission on Protecting and Reducing Public Secrecy, which had been looking into declassifying a mass of material dealing with Soviet espionage in the United States gathered over the previous fifty years, a secret archive known as the Venona project. "Up until then, the Venona files were known to only a handful of people, Senator Moynihan being one of them," Brent said. "He suggested that we get together, then he invited John Haynes and Harvey Klehr down to Washington to testify before his commission. Why? What we had published in this book, which was based upon the opening up of the Soviet archives, were plain text originals of messages that had been encoded by Soviet cryptologists and sent to the Soviet embassy in Washington and the Soviet consulate in New York City. And here the very same material was classified top secret in the United States. They came to the conclusion that there was no reason to keep all of this secret over here when it was already being published by Yale University Press." The board's findings, presented to President Bill Clinton in 1997, included a recommendation that the Federal Bureau of Investigation release the Venona file, which was approved.

In the process of all this, Brent developed a friendship with Moynihan, and in 1998 Yale published his book *Secrecy: The American Experience.* In it, Moynihan wrote that the "secrecy system" in the United States, as he called it, had "systematically denied American historians access to the records of American history. Of late we find ourselves relying on archives of the former Soviet Union in Moscow to resolve questions of what was going on in Washington at mid-century." The Venona intercepts, Moynihan affirmed, "contained overwhelming proof of the activities of Soviet spy networks in America, complete with names, dates, places, and deeds." In addition to voicing public support for the Yale series, Moynihan put Brent in touch with other people who offered financial help. An early admirer of the project whose support proved critical was the conservative columnist and founder of the *National Review,* William F. Buckley, Jr., Class of 1951, who Brent said "helped me raise a great deal of money." Buckley's initial gesture of support came in one of his weekly columns, syndicated in two hundred newspapers around the country. "If you have influence," he told his readers, "use it to raise money for the Annals of Communism series of the Yale University Press, Jonathan Brent, Executive Editor, 302 Temple St., New Haven, Conn. 06520." The appeal produced immediate results, with money sent in from a multitude of sources, some as modest as a five-dollar-a-year contribution from a woman in Maryland, others as hefty as a fifty-thousand-dollar gift from a car dealer in Dallas, Texas. Major funding finally arrived as well, not surprisingly, given the nature of the explosive disclosures, from a number of conservative groups that included the John M. Olin Foundation, the Lynde and Harry Bradley Foundation, the William H. Donner Foundation, and the David Woods Kemper Memorial Foundation.

"I am so indebted to Bill Buckley," Brent said of the columnist, who died on February 27, 2008, at age eighty-two, several months after this interview was conducted. "He is a great, wonderful guy. People who think that Buckley is just an idealogue, they're wrong. He's a very loyal, good friend. He called me up one day, and after a long conversation, I told him, 'Mr. Buckley, we don't have a single thing politically in common.' He said not to worry, that was fine, it was the work that was important. The truth is, I don't care a whit about a person's politics. I'm constantly on the lookout for excellent pieces of well-written scholarship that tell the truth, that's my motivation." He noted that among his most recent authors was the well-known liberal writer Gore Vidal, whose *Inventing a Nation: Washington, Adams, Jefferson* was released in 2003 as part of the Icons of America series Brent established and which to date has sold more than 120,000 copies.

The ultimate significance of the Annals of Communism series, in Brent's mind, is that it brought the Press "to a whole different dimension as a publisher of recent history," and he offered it as an example of what university press publishing is capable of doing. "People come to me now and say, 'I can actually teach a course on this subject, because you publish these books.' What university publishing has is credibility, but along with credibility, scholarly publishing has the aura of specialization. Here's where that obscure word *vision* comes in, too, since this is not something that we just happened to slip into. We have done this quite consciously. So I ask this:

Whoever heard of the idea that scholarship is something that has to be of commercial value? To say that a scholarly program should be self-supporting is self-contradictory. So to my mind, that means then that somebody's got to pay for it. In the 1960s, there was a huge amount of government money to do exactly that. The Cold War kept the engines hot for American competitiveness and brought in a whole lot of public funding, and the libraries bought the books. Nowadays, they get together and buy one copy of a book and share it among themselves, even though a book costs more to publish now than it did twenty years ago. Well, somebody still has to pay for it. You can't get something for nothing."

Brent's passion for books is unmistakable, and innate, as it turns out. His father, Stuart Brent, was renowned in his time as one of the leading independent booksellers in the United States, a career he documented in *The Seven Stairs* (1962), a charming memoir published by Houghton Mifflin and named for Brent's first store in Chicago. When the operation moved from Rush Street to Michigan Avenue, the business was renamed Stuart Brent Books and was well known as a meeting place for the literati, with people like Saul Bellow, Nelson Algren, and Studs Terkel among the frequent visitors. It closed in 1995. "I grew up in the basement of my father's bookstore, surrounded by piles of *Partisan Review,* and the idea that all the fun was going on upstairs is an important one for me," Brent said. "Jean-Paul Sartre and Simone de Beauvoir came through, signed copies of their books, Duke Ellington came through, Tennessee Williams, Gore Vidal. I didn't know who they were, but it didn't make any difference, they were up-stairs, and I wanted to be up there with them. To me, this is what publishing is. It isn't just books, it's a life. It's all about getting upstairs and joining the party. And that came out of my sitting in the basement of my father's store when I was six years old. That is what publishing is. If you take that away from publishing, you have a completely sterile, meaningless sort of non-interesting world."

For all the critical acclaim the Annals of Communism has received, it has not lacked detractors. "Believe me, that series has upset a lot of apple carts," Frank Turner told me. "Let's just say that there are people who would rather live with their illusions. A series like that has not always been welcomed by the larger academic community. But you've got to have editors like Jon Brent, or like Ed Tripp before him, who will push the envelope in ways that mean that, at the end of the day, you end up with a series of books that make a dif-ference. And that's something that Tripp did and something that Brent has done."

The Annals of Communism was not the only high-profile series undertaken during John Ryden's tenure and not the only project to require a massive infusion of outside funding and the hiring of teams of scholars to do the work. A few months before Jonathan Brent was thinking about making a trip to Moscow in 1991, the Press announced, amid considerable fanfare, the formation of a collaboration with the American

Council of Learned Societies and the China International Publishing Group to publish a series of books on China representing the best of both Western and Chinese scholarship, each produced in both English and Chinese. The first book to appear in the Culture and Civilization of China series was *Three Thousand Years of Chinese Painting,* a spectacular production that included more than three hundred color plates and featured chapters by six prominent scholars of Chinese art. Three of the authors—Yang Xin, deputy director of the Palace Museum in Beijing, Nie Chongzheng, a research fellow at the museum, and Lang Shaojun, director at the Institute of Fine Arts of the Chinese Academy of Arts in Beijing—were Chinese; the others—Richard M. Barnhart, a professor of art history at Yale, James Cahill, emeritus professor of art history at the University of California at Berkeley, and Wu Hung, a professor of Chinese art history at the University of Chicago—were American. The pictorial art represented everything from cave petroglyphs of ancient sun priests to naturalistic depictions of World War II refugees.

To launch the release of the first book in October 1997, Ryden traveled to China and spoke at the Great Hall of the People in Beijing. "It was a big event, with many senior officials in attendance," he said shortly after his return to the United States. "I told them that our hope with this series is to create a university without walls. It is necessary to understand the long and complicated history of this people. A lack of understanding is a dangerous thing." Later that month, President

Jiang Zemin of China brought a number of advance copies of the English edition to Washington and gave them as presents to President Bill Clinton, Vice President Al Gore, and several leaders in Congress. Other titles released since then include: *Chinese Architecture* (2002), *Key Concepts in Chinese Philosophy* (2002), *Balanced Discourses* (2002), *The Formation of Chinese Civilization: An Archaeological Perspective* (2005), and *Chinese Sculpture* (2006). More than half a million dollars was necessary to fund just the first book, which involved dozens of collaborators on both sides of the Pacific and took six years to produce. Projected at first to produce seventy-five titles within twenty-five years, the series has since been cut back to more modest goals, though three new titles, on Chinese calligraphy, ceramics, and textiles, were under way as Yale entered its centennial year in 2008.

Looking back on the eventful years of his directorship, Ryden said it was impossible to single out any one book that brought him the most satisfaction, and chose instead to reflect on the process itself, not on individual titles. "The things that loom large in my memory are variously about the publishing of books, rather than the books themselves," he said. "If there is one thing that ties them all together, it is growth. Growth and change were the one constant, and the growing and adaptation pains that accompanied them. The list grew constantly; there was hardly a year when the number of titles we published didn't increase." And in the process of expanding the list, he added, "we were doing a lot of learning on the job.

We were learning how to publish textbooks, how to publish reference books, how to be better paperback publishers, how to publish electronically, how to publish trade books—all the while trying to figure out how to continue to publish for the ever-declining library market."

One of the biggest and most unexpected challenges he faced as director came in the fall of 1984 during a ten-week strike of 2,600 clerical and technical workers at the university that affected every department on campus. "Roughly half of our staff was on the picket line," Ryden said. "The rest—editors, marketers, designers, managers—took on, in addition to their own everyday work of acquiring and making and selling books, everything from filling orders and shipping and wrapping books to shoveling snow. It was a crash course in publishing. It was damn hard work. And it cost us, though no one could ever say how much, maybe a million dollars in books that didn't get acquired or that didn't get sold. It was close, but we survived. The fall 1985 list—the books that somehow got signed up and edited and produced during that year—was one of our strongest ever, and was a huge success."

As the Press grew, the building at 302 Temple Street became terribly overcrowded, with staff working in makeshift accommodations in various campus locations at considerable cost and loss of effectiveness. That problem was solved in 1992 with construction of the Evans Wing, named for the principal donor, Edward P. Evans, Class of 1964, whose capital campaign gift of one million dollars—and an additional challenge grant of $250,000—made the project possible. Among other gifts was $125,000 from the Kingsley Trust Association, the parent organization of Scroll and Key, which had underwritten the Yale Shakespeare six decades earlier. The fourteen-thousand-square-foot addition, designed by the architect Cesar Pelli, doubled the working space of the Press.

A smooth entry into the highly competitive world of trade publishing was made possible in 2001 by the formation of a joint enterprise with Harvard University Press and MIT Press to share distribution of their titles. "To succeed at trade and paperback publishing, it was necessary to respond to the needs of a changing and volatile marketplace—to take risks, to put money up front, to push books through the pipeline in a timely fashion, and to be able to move stock and fulfill orders rapidly and accurately," Ryden recalled. The person who has supervised Yale's participation in the enterprise from the beginning, John Rollins, worked with his counterparts in Massachusetts to organize TriLiteral LLC, a limited liability partnership, and to build a 155,000-square-foot distribution center in Cumberland, Rhode Island. "We simply outgrew our warehouse," Rollins told me. "It just so happened that MIT and Harvard were having the same growth problems at the same time, so we decided to go in together, and together we were able to afford a bigger, more modern, more technologically savvy sort of operation." TriLiteral was established and delegated the task of managing from one central location the distribution of every book and journal for all three presses, which together account for more than fifteen thousand active titles. By May 2002, the listings of all three were in one database, a considerable advantage, since each share many of the same customers. TriLiteral can ship up to three thousand orders per day, a figure that equates to more than 26,000 individual volumes and journals. The warehouse can accommodate 7.6 million volumes. Underscoring the profound changes that have taken place in the marketing of the Press's intellectual product, Rollins noted that over the five-year period from fiscal 2003 to the end of fiscal 2007, online retail sales increased by more than 270 percent.

Like Chester Kerr a generation before him, Ryden expressed special gratitude to members of the Publications Committee, singling out by name the following faculty members, who, he said, "were of inestimable value" to him during his two-decade tenure: Akhil Amar, Marie Borroff, Ralph S. Brown, Guido Calabresi, Donald J. Cohen, Kai Erikson, Alan E. Kazdin, Jaroslav Pelikan, Alison F. Richard, James C. Scott, Albert J. Solnit, Frank M. Turner, and Harry H. Wellington. He extended his gratitude also to book professionals from the publishing industry who served on the Board of Governors while he was director: George Brockway, Thomas H. Guinzburg, Lawrence Hughes, Donald S. Lamm, Tim Rix, Jack Schulman, Anthony M. Schulte, Morgan K. Smith, and Peter Workman.

When Ryden announced in March 2002 that he would

be retiring as director of the Press, President Richard Levin lauded his work in a letter to the staff, focusing on his accomplishments over the previous twenty-three years. "During this time the Press has published more than 4,000 books, two-thirds of all the books published during its ninety-four-year history. Its publications have won more than 500 prizes, including the Pulitzer and Bancroft prizes, the Mitchell prizes in art, the Christian Gauss award of Phi Beta Kappa and the Ralph Waldo Emerson award." Choosing from all the titles published to highlight some individually was a daunting prospect, one that Levin declined to do, except to note the extraordinary range and versatility of what had been accomplished during Ryden's years in the first-floor corner office:

> Over the years Yale University Press has developed four publishing lines that overlap with and complement its core mission: an art list; a general trade list; a reference list; and a text or educational list. It publishes scholarly books of imaginative and influential scholarship, biographies, interpretive histories, chronicles, reference books, books on the world's "hot spots," books by statesmen and artists, reference works, encyclopedias, companions, handbooks, guides, teaching materials in thirty modern and ancient and foreign languages from Arabic through Yoruba, multimedia programs, interactive computer based materials, and more than ninety different series. And these are just the general categories. During Mr. Ryden's stewardship the growth of these lines increased

the size of the list and in turn financed the expansion of the whole publishing program, more than doubling the number of monographs and licensed editions published annually.

Or, put another way, what Levin was saying, essentially, is that John Ryden had made sure Yale did everything a scholarly publisher is supposed to do, and then some. In the process, he was able to balance his bottom line by virtue of having "enriched the mix," a strategy that continues to inform Press activities as it proceeds into its second century of operation.

FOUR

A Press in Transition

OR THOSE WHO ARE STIRRED BY
the majesty of books, a walk through the
George Parmly Day Room in the headquarters of Yale University Press is an
exercise in humility. The elegant building
at 302 Temple Street that contains it was
designed in 1840 by the renowned architect Ithiel Town to be
the residence of a New Haven merchant and was acquired in
1890 by the United Church on the Green for use as a parish
hall; a spacious chapel in the rear—a rectangular enclosure
with an arching cathedral ceiling—was erected shortly thereafter. When the Press took up residence in 1973, editorial offices
were installed in a series of open alcoves on two levels along
the exterior walls, with wooden bookcases erected in each
compartment to showcase what is today a century's worth of
scholarly achievement, more than eight thousand titles shelved
chronologically according to their year of publication.

Because volumes are not categorized here by author or subject, the full range and richness of Press activity over ten decades is apparent in one sweeping panorama. A browser poking randomly through the stacks might pause halfway into the continuum to find grouped together in one corner such titles as *The Scientific Age: The Impact of Science on Society,* by L. V. Berkner; *Direct Use of the Sun's Energy,* by Farrington Daniels; *Character Text for Beginning Chinese,* by John De-Francis; *England's Earliest Protestants, 1520–1535,* by William A. Clebsch; *The Autobiography of Benjamin Franklin,* edited by Leonard W. Labaree; *Wordsworth's Poetry, 1787–1814,* by Geoffrey H. Hartman; *Village in Vietnam,* by Gerald Cannon Hickey; *German Social Democracy, 1918–1933,* by Richard N. Hunt; *Town Planning in London: The Eighteenth and Nineteenth Centuries,* by Donald J. Olsen; and *The Emergence of Biological Organization,* by Henry Quastler—their only point in common being that each bears the same imprint on the copyright page and that each was published in one year, in this instance 1964. A similar pattern prevails for all the other years of Press history.

It is in this majestic room, too, that the Publications Committee gathers regularly to discuss the various proposals and manuscripts under consideration and to ponder the direction and evolving mission of the Press itself. At a typical meeting, the long conference table in the center is decked out with copies of recently issued books, a dramatic touch that reinforces, in a very visual way, the end result of academic publishing at the highest levels of accomplishment. For an outsider such as myself who has read through the minutes of these gatherings from the past hundred years, it was an eye-opening experience to sit through a couple of them and to see firsthand how strategies are developed. A whole lexicon of categories for books in various stages of preparation took on a sharper focus as well. Proposals, for instance, are rarely approved outright on first hearing. Most projects that reach this stage have already gone through an initial vetting and have editors from the staff championing their merits, so summary rejections here are extremely rare, though there is a spirited discussion that takes place, after which some are "encouraged," others "greatly encouraged." In the case of manuscripts, where committee members are expected to have already read reports submitted by outside readers—that anxious phase of scrutiny known as "peer review"—some may be sent back for further retooling, others accepted enthusiastically for publication. Occasionally a manuscript will be approved provisionally, "pending further reading reports and appropriate author response." It is not unusual for the committee to consider several dozen projects-in-progress at these meetings, though usually there is other business to discuss as well. On the docket for the two I attended in November and December 2006 was the whole concept of scholarly publishing itself, a pressing issue that has taken on a sense of urgency at every university press in the United States.

Mission statements, as I noted in chapter 2, are very

important among university presses, and they are constantly being tweaked as times change and conditions warrant. John E. Donatich, who succeeded John Ryden as director of the Press in 2003, has committed himself to keeping Yale at the forefront of innovation and to developing dynamic projects for the Press to pursue in the twenty-first century. With that in mind, he had asked members of the Publications Committee to think about ways to formulate "a set of criteria for excellence in scholarly writing" and to share them at the December 2006 meeting. He asked members to think in particular about the "crisis" that has enveloped scholarly publishing over the past decade, and for background, he suggested they read a pertinent essay published in the *New Republic* a few months earlier by David A. Bell, a professor of history at Johns Hopkins, titled "The Bookless Future: What the Internet Is Doing to Scholarship." Donatich proposed, for starters, that the committee initiate a continuing discussion that might form "the beginning of a new typology," one centered on a consideration of just what, exactly, defines a "monograph," and try to agree on ways to determine when a monograph can be said to have achieved such excellence that it becomes a "gem of scholarship."

The difference between the two—especially the idea of what constitutes a monograph—has engendered a variety of definitions throughout scholarly publishing. A particular favorite of mine is a distinction put forth by David Bromwich, Sterling Professor of English at Yale and, since 2004, chairman of the Publications Committee. "A monograph," he told his colleagues at one meeting, with tongue clearly in cheek, "is a work of scholarship that will not sell many copies until it does, at which point it becomes a gem of scholarship." When I asked Bromwich for a favorite example, he named Louis Martz's *Poetry of Meditation* (1954) as a top choice, describing it as a work at first perceived to be a highly specialized study of decidedly limited interest but one that "over a couple of generations picked up a lot of readers" and has remained vibrant to this day. Perhaps the most dramatic example of a Yale release that achieved such coveted stature is *The Lonely Crowd*, the David Riesman book that is a cornerstone on the backlist six decades after it first appeared in print with minimal sales expectations. For the purposes of discussion among his colleagues, Donatich thought that it might be useful to analyze what qualities the monograph and the "gem of scholarship" might share (like original primary research, disciplinary progress, rigorous methodology, intricate conceptualization, compound argument, and substantive scholarly apparatus) and what characteristics might distinguish them. Although the monograph has always been responsible, professional, and intended for peer groups and specialists, the gem of scholarship, he suggested, is sometimes speculative or risk-taking and aspires to satisfy not only peers but a wider educated group of readers. Yale University Press books to achieve both sets of criteria over the years have included *Interaction of Color*, by Josef Albers; *The Rise and Decline of Nations*, by Mancur Olson;

The Stripping of the Altars, by Eamon Duffy; and *American Judaism: A History,* by Jonathan D. Sarna.

At the December 11, 2006, meeting, the discussion pursued a number of avenues. One member suggested that there is often "a huge conceptual leap" between a doctoral dissertation and an author's first book and that because "the skill of writing great books needs to be honed," middle-aged and older people "are often the best suited" for scholarly writing. Another member acknowledged "the need to be careful about people making the leap between the dissertation and the first book," but stressed how important it is "for the Press to have these first books" and that the "Press should be in the business of not just publishing books, but also publishing authors" at the beginning of hopeful careers. Yet another member asked if there were any figures to indicate how many submissions actually become published books. Donatich replied that fewer than 2 percent of submissions to the Press make it to the Publications Committee for approval, joking that even Yale College admits 9 percent of its freshman applicants. Jonathan Brent offered the view that "what matters to the Press is who would value the book if it were published." He gave as an example an "excellent book" he was then reviewing on Eastern European music. "Because the Press loses money whenever it publishes books of this nature," he said, "the editors must decide which ones are the best, and who needs them."

The point to all this, Donatich would elaborate to me later during one of several interviews we had for this book, is fundamental and provides, in a way, a gateway to the kind of writing that he would like to see the Press publish in the years to come. One way he plans to do this, he told me, is to work toward a reorganization of priorities that remains mindful of the fact that "we are really several different kinds of publishers," first and foremost an academic publisher that takes on projects strictly on the basis of scholarly merit, regardless of sales potential—and which, he stressed, comprise the vast majority of titles published in a given year—and a trade publisher, where sales potential is very much a factor in the decision-making process. "That's very straightforward," he said. "If it's a trade book, the only reason to publish it is because it is a work of excellence and broad appeal with a crossover audience. There are books where we will sell only three to five hundred copies, and that means they have to be supported by our endowment or from other sources. We do this because we honor our mission. That's our covenant."

Donatich said that a lot of soul-searching has been taking place to consider the evolving role of a university press in a constantly changing environment of declining book sales and increased reliance among students and researchers on electronic media. "One of the essential questions that we are now required to consider is that we take a look at what absolutely *needs* to be a book," he said. "I think what the electronic alternative has done throughout the industry is to raise the bar up a little bit in deciding what ultimately needs to be between hard covers. So then you ask, 'What are the things that make a book?' There are a number of things to think about, and it's not just market. Is there a seamless narrative drive to it? Does the author lay out and interweave several complex arguments in service of an underlying theory? Is the passion of the research, that kind of passion that is almost visceral in the text, matched by formal invention? Or when a master scholar is juggling fifteen different arguments, theoretical, empirical, and then is bringing them together in a very artful way, and they are completely interdependent, that needs to be a book, too. What doesn't need to be a book is incremental research in a certain discipline. Something like that might just as well be a journal article."

A graduate of New York University in 1982, with a master's degree summa cum laude from New York University, Donatich came to Yale from Basic Books, a trade house well known for the kind of nonfiction that enjoys the dual distinction of being scholarly sound and readily accessible to general readers; he spent seven years there as publisher and vice president. From 1992 to 1996, Donatich held a variety of positions at HarperCollins, including vice president and director of product and marketing development, and he held similar positions with the Putnam Publishing Group before that. His writing credits include numerous articles and essays for *Atlantic Monthly, Harper's,* the *Nation,* and the *Village Voice* and an erudite reflection on his first becoming a father, *Ambivalence, a Love Story: Portrait of a Marriage,* published in 2005.

To celebrate the Press's centenary in 2008, Donatich will

host an academic conference jointly sponsored by the Whitney Center for the Humanities and the Beinecke Library called "Why the Book Matters" in which publishers, scholars, and writers from around the country will gather to argue what he calls "the counterintuitive case that the Age of Information, in which access to research and data is ubiquitous, is an age that argues for the central importance of the book. And, by extension, for the publisher. In the process of selection, development, editing, design, and distribution, publishers provide the culture with a gatekeeping standard of excellence that is needed more now than ever."

Over the first five years of Donatich's tenure as director (he was signed to a second five-year contract in 2007), the Press has published, on average, 320 books a year, 200 of them in hardcover, the remainder in paperback. Of these, most are works of scholarship, as any examination of the seasonal lists bears out. Though comparatively few in number, titles earmarked for the trade sector have nonetheless performed in ways that allow the Press to fulfill the scholarly goals it has set itself. A few figures from recent years are informative. Between 2002 and 2007, the Press has had three books whose total sales each eclipsed the one hundred thousand figure, Edmund Morgan's *Benjamin Franklin* (2002), Gore Vidal's *Inventing a Nation: Washington, Adams, Jefferson* (2003), and E. H. Gombrich's *Little History of the World* (2005). A further breakdown of the three most recent years yields the following:

In 2005, John C. Bogle's *Battle for the Soul of Capitalism*

sold more than fifteen thousand copies in hardcover and another ten thousand in the paperback edition that was released
the following year. Books that sold ten thousand or more copies: *In the Company of Crows and Ravens,* by John M. Marzluff
and Tony Angell; *The Encyclopedia of New England,* edited by
Burt Feintuch and David H. Watters; *The Hudson: A History,*
by Tom Lewis; and *Chanel,* edited by Harold Koda and Andrew Bolton. *The Unknown Battle of Midway: The Destruction
of the American Torpedo Squadrons,* by Alvin Kernan, surpassed
five thousand copies.

In 2006, five books accounted for sales that would be
welcome at any commercial house. Topping the list were *Green
to Gold: How Smart Companies Use Environmental Strategy to
Innovate, Create Value, and Build Competitive Advantage,* by
Daniel C. Esty and Andrew S. Winston, forty thousand copies
in hardcover, and *America at the Crossroads: Democracy, Power,
and the Neoconservative Legacy,* by Francis Fukuyama, thirty
thousand copies. Weighing in at twenty thousand: *Caesar:
Life of a Colossus,* by Adrian Goldsworthy; *An Anthology of
Graphic Fiction, Cartoons, and True Stories,* edited by Ivan Bru-
netti; and *The Yale Book of Quotations,* by Fred R. Shapiro. Two
books surpassed the ten-thousand-copy plateau, *Manliness,* by
Harvey C. Mansfield, and *In the Studio: Visits with Contemporary Cartoonists,* by Todd Hignite. Rounding out the Yale
best-seller list for the year was *Empires of the Atlantic World:
Britain and Spain in America, 1492–1830,* by J. H. Elliott, at
five thousand copies.

In 2007, *The Occupation of Iraq: Winning the War, Losing the Peace,* by Ali A. Allawi, topped the sales list at twenty thousand copies, followed by seven releases with ten thousand or more copies each: *Two Lives: Gertrude and Alice,* by Janet Malcolm; *Shakespeare the Thinker,* by A. D. Nuttall; *Bound Together: How Traders, Preachers, Adventurers, and Warriors Shaped Globalization,* by Nayan Chanda; *Stanley: The Impossible Life of Africa's Greatest Explorer,* by Tim Jeal; *Fallen Angels,* by Harold Bloom; *The Last Human: A Guide to Twenty-Two Species of Extinct Humans,* created by G. J. Sawyer and Viktor Deak, with text by Esteban Sarmiento, G. J. Sawyer, and Richard Milner and contributions from Donald C. Johanson, Meave Leakey, and Ian Tattersall; and *Amazing Rare Things: The Art of Natural History in the Age of Discovery,* by David Attenborough, Susan Owens, Martin Clayton, and Rea Alexandratos.

During this period, three Press books won the Bancroft Prize, given annually by Columbia University for outstanding work in nonfiction: Alan Gallay, *The Indian Slave Trade: The Rise of the English Empire in the American South, 1670–1717* (2002), George M. Marsden, *Jonathan Edwards: A Life* (2003), and Erskine Clarke, *Dwelling Place: A Plantation Epic* (2005). In 2007, John H. Elliott received the Francis Parkman Award from the Society of American Historians for *Empires of the Atlantic World.*

In another apparent concession to changing times and shifting reading habits, the Yale staff has been actively looking to supplement its lists with books that can be read easily in a couple of sittings, using several recent endeavors in the trade as models. The premise is basic enough. "There is every reason to believe that the opportunity to write a short book for a prestigious list, on a subject about which one is passionate, will be extremely attractive to a broad range of writers, especially public intellectuals who wish to bring their influence to bear through concise argument," Donatich wrote in one outline of his plan. "The books will be 40,000 to 45,000 words in length, and will be published in a small trim size." One recent Yale effort along these lines, Gore Vidal's *Inventing a Nation*, served as a prototype; it was acquired by Jonathan Brent to initiate a series he called Icons of America, and was published during Donatich's first year as director. Two other "iconic" works released in 2008 were a social history of the hamburger, by Josh Ozersky, online food editor for *New York Magazine*, and *Wall Street: America's Dream Palace*, by Steve Fraser, a historian whose books include *Every Man a Speculator: A History of Wall Street in American Life*. To launch a conceptual series called Why X Matters—the idea being that an intriguing subject is paired with an interesting author—the Press commissioned Elisabeth Young-Bruehl, author of a 1982 biography for Yale, *Hannah Arendt: For Love of the World*, to write *Why Arendt Matters;* released in 2006, it was named among the "best of the best of university presses" for the year by the Association of American University Presses. "Ideally," Donatich wrote, "these books will have a kind of chemical reaction by the virtue of assigning Subject X to Writer W who matters on X." Future volumes in the series include *Why Poetry Matters*, by Jay Parini (2008); *Why Africa Matters*, by the Nobel laureate Wole Soyinka; *Why Architecture Matters*, by the *New Yorker* writer Paul Goldberger; and *Why Translation Matters*, by Edith Grossman.

These days, perfectly respectable books that have a modicum of success in the marketplace—but may not be profitable enough to satisfy the business expectations of a large commercial house—have become fair game for publishers whose financial expectations are much less demanding. This very subject came up during a long luncheon conversation I had in 2005 at the Graduate Faculty Club with John Hollander, critic, editor, translator, Sterling Professor of English at Yale, MacArthur Fellow, and a poet whose own first collection, *A Crackling of Thorns*, was selected in 1958 by W. H. Auden as a winner in the Yale Series of Younger Poets. The thrust of our general conversation, of course, was poetry, but also how so few outlets exist today for its publication and the example Yale sets in providing a forum for emerging voices.

"This is a toehold into an increasingly interesting question, which is how so much of what used to be trade publishing can only be done by a nonprofit today," Hollander said, and he was basing his comments on opinions drawn from having published seventeen books of his own over the past half-century in a variety of outlets, commercial as well as academic. "There have been excellent models for what used to be high-level trade publishing that have now become mid-scale trade publishing by university presses. I think university presses can and should publish very good books which aren't being published any more by the trade. Let's remember that in the 1950s through the 1960s, all sorts of books in the field of literature—books that would be published subsequently by university presses—were published only by the trade. I fully believe that a lot of what had once been good trade publishing may now have to be done by the nonprofits. Trade publishers used to be able to be bare profit, but since they've all been taken over by various foreign conglomerates, they aren't interested in the borderline books. If a university press can make marginal profit or simply cover costs, then it's doing what it's supposed to do. A book that can sell four thousand copies in hardcover—that's a big sale for a university press. I was just delighted when you told me that Yale Press made a profit last year. If it makes a profit, that's wonderful—but it can't be profit making. If it's in the black, that means it can afford to do some other wonderful things. That's what being in the black is for, to be able to do those other things. Black subsidizes the red, and it levels out."

David Bromwich, chairman of the Publications Committee, was clear in his interview with me about what he feels should be the role of a university press in the twenty-first century. "I think it should be considered the publishing backbone of intellectual life," he said. "So I am for keeping intellectually serious academic presses that way. I also think it's important

that Yale University Press be on the map and have its reputation in such good order that its books are known. Yale Press
books now are very nicely noticed in the *New York Times* and
other places. On the other hand, it's not a for-profit organization." Having said that, he acknowledged that the Press
manages to operate in the black, which, he allowed, "is a tricky
balance" to maintain. In a similar vein, he also emphasized that
the type of books the Press seeks to acquire for its trade division should not be regarded as "intellectually inferior" in any
way. "To my knowledge, we have never approved a book that
people thought was trash or was lacking in the relevant areas
of learning, but we have approved popular books, including
some that persons on the board thought were written down
in such a way that they wouldn't do it themselves. There are
occasional books like that, while on the other hand we have
approved books that are written too much in the jargon of
a given field of study, whether it's sociology or economics,
whatever. Our editors try to work with that, and try to bring
the language into some recognizable shape. But I think that
continues to be a problem."

Clearly a person with a flair for lively phrasing, Bromwich offered yet another thought on a category of book that
is not purely academic and not entirely commercial either. "I
regard books like this in a middle category of not-runaway-
best-sellers," he said. Choosing not to identify any by title,
he offered a general description. "They're good enough in a
scholarly way. They're felt to have an audience—and they sell

decently, and by that I mean they sell better than most scholarly books. That's an example of that middle category." But the fundamental mission of the Press, he insisted, remains fairly clear, regardless of how people might feel on either side of the discussion. "To tell you the truth, I don't think the expectation is right on either side, either from the academic perspective, where there is a sense that the Press should just publish what we—the academics—are doing, or from a Press perspective, where the argument might be that the public has rejected the present shape of academic discourse, so we have to refine the paradigm. Unfortunately, it is an overprofessionalized, obscure system we have here. Where are they going to go for authors? At the end of the day, they're going to go to scholars. And where are the scholars? In universities." Bromwich said he sees wisdom in "putting on the brakes when necessary, and hoping to have good trade books for the next list," but added that he regards the balance now as being "about right," with one caveat: "I don't think we need to go all out for the dollars, to go entirely for the reader. I think the statement of mission of the Press is pretty clear: it says something about the idea of promoting free inquiry and representing what is most worthwhile in learning in the various fields, somewhat overlapping with the curriculum. That is something we have to always keep in mind."

Donatich told me that while he does not think a university press should be required by mandate to support the curriculum of its parent institution in any strict sense, it does have an obligation to "mirror the strengths" of its academic programs and to draw on the specialties of key and influential faculty, with notable examples to be found in the fields of history and art. As to whether a university press should regard as one of its responsibilities the publication of dissertations, Donatich said he favors a case-by-case evaluation. "It depends on quality, it depends on scope, it depends on maturity and on promise. I think that when a dissertation shows some promise of a scholar at the beginning of a great career, you want to be a part of that. You don't worry if it sells three or four hundred copies, because you have other books on your list that are carrying the weight and making that kind of title something you can justify and do. Our editorial decision-making process has little in common with the hiring or tenure-granting considerations at Yale except for the overriding obsession with quality." Coincidental with this conversation was the approval at the November 2006 Publications Committee meeting I attended of two revised dissertations for release by the Press.

Implicit in any consideration of how scholarly publishing is evolving is the changing nature of scholarship itself. "There are a lot of people who sort of take a look at how scholarship matters in the world, and they reach out," Donatich said. "The Yale faculty is a perfect illustration of that," he added, offering as an example John Lewis Gaddis, professor of military and naval history, declared by the *New York Times* to be the "dean" of Cold War historians. "Yale has a lot of people like

Gaddis—Edmund Morgan and Paul Kennedy are a couple of others who spring to mind—who are often on the op-ed pages of the leading newspapers and who are often profiled in popular magazines, whose opinion and guidance often appear in *Current Affairs*. These are examples of scholarship going outside the immediate world of scholars, and that is consistent with the approach we are trying to take with the Press. I like to think that our activity should be almost as various as the university's activity. So while most of our work will involve the kind of research-driven content that might make it into a graduate seminar, every once in a while there will be a book that's done more or less for pleasure. I think the lighter side of our list has a real place too, and I also think we want to be a one-shop publisher for a lot of scholars. A lot of scholars don't have the old ambivalence about wanting to be public intellectuals as well as top-notch scholars. So there are two aspects of their intellectual life. One is the joy of doing pure research; the other is having the impact of public intellectual work."

Another prime example of such a scholar is Jonathan Spence, whose association with the Press spans five decades and who has written most of his books for trade publishers. The idea of identifying a target readership means a great deal to him and is an especially pertinent concept to grasp for any academic publisher that hopes to survive in the current climate. "I think the Press is always aware of the presence of some kind of audience, or the lack of one," he stressed in one of the first interviews I conducted for this book. "They do need to have people read their books, after all, and if possible to buy them, maybe not on the scale of trade books, but even non-profits have to break even in some way or another." One way of assuring this is to have "two or three titles each year which can carry a lot of much lower-selling monographic studies," he said. Yet for all that juggling of material, Spence added, "scholarship is still very hard to gauge," and he cited his own work as an example. Around the time that Yale published his first book, *Ts'ao Yin and the K'ang-hsi Emperor: Bondservant and Master,* in 1966, Spence said he began to consider writing for a broader audience, especially as a number of trade publishers approached him with invitations to write for them. "I got interested in the interconnection between scholarship and the more general readership. I used to ask myself why scholarship had to be arcane. That may be the wrong question to ask, but that's how I phrased it myself. My feeling was this: that instead of spending years and years on the research and then just trying to write it up and get somebody to take it, supposing you spent half the time on the research and half the time on the writing? Just really concentrate on that; just shut yourself away and go on and do it—and then see who wants to publish it and who wants to read it. That's what I did. I got involved in a different world."

Spence's involvement in that "different world," as he called it, has earned him recognition as one of the foremost scholars of Chinese civilization from the sixteenth century to the present while at the same time allowing him to reach an appreciative following outside the academy. In 1969, Little, Brown published *To Change China: Western Advisers in China, 1620–1960*. His other publishing credits include *The Death of Woman Wang* (1978), *The Gate of Heavenly Peace: The Chinese and Their Revolution, 1895–1980* (1981), *The Memory Palace of Matteo Ricci* (1984), and *Return to Dragon Mountain: Memories of a Late Ming Man* (2007), all with Viking; *Chan's Great Continent: China in Western Minds* (1998) and *The Search for Modern China* (1999), both with W. W. Norton; and *The Question of Hu* (1988), with Alfred A. Knopf. "Some of this, I guess, was straightforwardly financial," he said, though he stressed his overriding commitment "to write in a way that any person of education can understand it."

These experiences have imbued Spence with a strong sense of just what a university press should strive to accomplish. "I think one of the things it should be is a guardian of genuine standards, of excellence, of making something based on true research scholarship available. One could add to that, making it available to professionals, or one could bracket that and say, to the interested public—and there is, of course, an enormous difference between the two. But I think a university press should be the keeper of really strong standards, and that it should try *not* to publish books that have enormous gaps in their evidential structures. I see, too, as an important goal to have at intervals speculative books that are declared to be speculative." On the matter of publishing faculty dissertations,

Spence said that "occasionally a dissertation is a wonderful book" and warrants publication.

For all the discussion about evolving functions and declining sales to libraries on standing order, the dark cloud that hangs over every university press today is the role electronic publishing will play in determining future projects. When Donatich and I were discussing the future of the Press, the conversation turned inevitably to whether he envisioned the creation of a Yale book that is entirely digital and not merely the electronic version of a printed book. "We will get there eventually, I suppose, but I think more likely there will have to be a very short run hardcover book with some digital long life to it." The Press has been involved in one experimental program as publisher of a set of CDs in what is known as the Perseus Project, an electronic compilation of source material and illustrations gathered by a team of scholars at Tufts University under the editorial direction of Gregory Crane. The first installment, *Perseus 1.0: Interactive Sources and Studies on Ancient Greece,* appeared in 1991; *Perseus 2.0,* about four times larger, was published in 1996. Since then, two new editions have been available online only.

A number of other presses have taken aggressive roles in trying to develop publishing programs that are "born digital," a gentle way of saying producing works that begin their existence, not on paper, but in the zeroes and ones of binary data. Among those at the forefront of these endeavors is Columbia University Press, which in 1999 established Gutenberg-e, a project that makes available on an open-access Web site scholarly monographs produced digitally in collaboration with the American Historical Association; twenty titles have been released through 2007. Coordinated by the American Council of Learned Societies, the Electronic Publishing Initiative at Columbia is funded partly by the Andrew W. Mellon Foundation, which contributed three million dollars to create what is called the History E-Book Project. Nine other university presses—University of California, Harvard, Johns Hopkins, MIT, University of Michigan, New York University, University of North Carolina, Oxford, and Rutgers—are actively involved as well. Meanwhile, officials at Rice University Press, which suspended operations entirely in 1996 owing to financial shortfalls, announced in 2006 that it was resuming operations as the nation's "first fully digital academic press," one that the university's president, David Leebron, predicted will provide "a solution for scholars—particularly those in the humanities—who are limited by the dearth of university presses."

At Yale, a $1.3 million grant from the Mellon Foundation announced in January 2008 will be used to develop a digital documentary edition of Stalin's personal archive, an outgrowth of the Annals of Communism series that will make available to scholars worldwide primary source materials and documents. Part of the program to be developed will be software that allows authors and researchers to transcribe, translate, and annotate the materials online without having to handle the originals in Moscow. A fully digitized version of all the documents contained in the massive archive is expected to be available on the World Wide Web by 2012.

All of these new projects—Icons of America, Why X Matters, the digital initiatives—take into account the need for the Press to be nimble. "I think there's a new respect for the fact that we are really several different kinds of publishers, and that we have to operate within each of these sets of circumstances," Donatich said. In addition to the various series that he hopes to establish within the trade group are several others that will go forward on the academic side. When I first discussed this prospect with Donatich, two programs in particular— a Yale Drama Series to be established along the lines of the Yale Younger Poets Series, and a World Republic of Letters Series that would seek out important works of literature in foreign languages to be translated and published in English editions—were in the final stages of planning. Both were still awaiting the most essential element of all—significant outside funding—to get off the ground. In each instance, donors had already been identified, but finer points still remained to be resolved. By the middle of 2007, both projects had been announced and were well under way.

The competition for playwrights, christened the Yale Drama Series, is sponsored jointly by the Press and Yale Repertory Theatre and is funded by a one-million-dollar grant from the David Charles Horn Foundation, established in 2005 by Francine Horn in memory of her late husband. David Horn was the publisher and CEO of *Here and There,* a forecasting and reporting publication that serves the fashion industry. The concept for the drama competition—which includes publication of the winning entry by the Press and a staged reading by Yale Repertory Theatre, plus a ten-thousand-dollar cash award—was proposed to Francine Horn by John Kulka, a senior editor at the Press from 2001 to 2007 and now executive editor at large for Harvard University Press. When Kulka and I spoke in 2006, preparations had advanced sufficiently that guidelines were being drawn for submissions and three-time Pulitzer Prize–winning playwright Edward Albee had agreed to serve as judge for the first two years of the competition. Kulka recalled for me how this particular endeavor had developed.

"Out of the blue I got a phone call one day, and this woman who I did not know at the time said, 'What can you do with a million dollars?' She then told me that it was her wish to honor her husband with something that would help aspiring writers. I said, 'Let me think about it, and let me give you a written proposal.' I had been thinking about do-ing something in the dramatic arts for a couple of reasons, because it seems to me—and I don't have an explanation as to why—that the dramatic arts are not really treated as a part of American literary culture. It's an oddity. I don't think Americans as a rule read plays. Moreover, playwrights are not really welcomed into the community of writers. Today, they're pretty much left on the margins of literary culture. So I thought here was a perfect opportunity to deal with this in a meaningful way, and the Younger Poets Series was already in place as a successful model to build on. I presented the idea to Mrs. Horn, and it took her all of three days to make up her mind."

Though the poetry series served as a prototype, there are several significant differences between the two competitions. Whereas the hopeful poets who submit manuscripts must be American citizens and must be forty years of age or younger, the drama competition has no age restrictions and is open to aspiring playwrights of any nationality. Thus it came to pass that on April 26, 2007, at ceremonies held in Lincoln Center in New York, Edward Albee presented the first David C. Horn Prize to an Irish citizen from Dublin who is a retired clinical psychologist. John Austin Connolly's play was selected from five hundred submissions for *The Boys from Siam*, a work based on the lives of Chang and Eng Bunker, the original "Siamese twins," who were joined throughout life at the sternum by a piece of cartilage. Much of the action of the play takes place on the day the twins died in 1874 at the age of sixty-two. Albee also announced the names of two runners-up, *The Secret Agenda of Trees*, by Colin McKenna, and *Open Rehearsal*, by Lazarre Seymour Simckes.

Another recent literature series, the Annotated Shakespeare, was launched in 2003, with fourteen plays released to date in paperback editions priced at $6.95 each. The series has been edited and annotated by Burton Raffel, Distinguished Professor of Arts and Humanities Emeritus and professor of

English emeritus at the University of Louisiana at Lafayette, and each play includes an afterword by Harold Bloom, Sterling Professor of Humanities at Yale. Raffel, who has published numerous books with trade and academic presses, a good number of them with Yale, had high praise in a conversation with me for the trend he has seen in recent years at the Press to "get over the barrier that scholarship has placed between itself and the rest of the world." Raffel said his idea for the Shakespeare series was to have texts that might explain "every word that it seemed to me that an undergraduate student would not know." John Kulka's concept for the series, Raffel said, was to "have a series that could be taught all the way down into high school, and I am pleased to hear that it is being used that way." The first title, issued in 2003, *Hamlet*, has sold more than thirty thousand copies to date; *Romeo and Juliet*, published the following year, was up to twenty-five thousand by the end of 2007.

Asked to identify his proudest accomplishments since coming to New Haven as director in 2003, Donatich pointed to two successes in particular. "I am very proud of the fact that I came to an organization that could inspire and manage a growth rate of 43 percent over the last five years—in a time of turmoil and downturn, no less. That explosive growth gave the Press a stabilizing organizational foundation and established us as the largest books-only, U.S.-based university press."

Another was the establishment of the Cecile and Theodore Margellos World Republic of Letters, an undertaking he had been thinking about for years and which was launched in 2007 with the announcement that several projects had been commissioned and would be published in time to commemorate the centennial of the Press in 2008. Not only does the project fill an egregious void in American publishing, but, Donatich said, it demonstrates the kind of cultural synergy that can come to full flower through the assistance of "a wonderful donor." In this instance, the benefactors are a couple who committed three million dollars to establish a foundation that will underwrite the translation and publication of literary fiction, poetry, drama, belles-lettres, and philosophy from Europe, Latin America, Africa, Asia, and the Middle East, works of great beauty and significance that otherwise would have no readership in the English-speaking world. "These are donors who wanted to do something with literature," Donatich said. "We proposed the concept, and it was a natural fit all around. Cecile Inglessis Margellos is a literary translator and critic herself with a great sensitivity to the art and challenges of translation, so this project has great native appeal to the family."

Theodore Margellos is managing director and cofounder of the Ilta Group, a private equity firm. The couple's daughter, Iliodora Margellos, is a member of the Yale College Class of 2006. In announcing the formation of the series, they said their "strongest belief is that Babel was a blessing, since each and every language reveals another vision of our world's infinite reality. Our dearest wish is, through great translation, to bring these visions together." The first books signed for the project include *Five Spice Street*, by Can Xue, a distinctive voice in contemporary Chinese fiction; *Songbook: The Selected Poems of Umberto Saba*, a new verse translation of the noted Italian poet's work; *The Selected Poems of Adonis*, a roundup of poems by an honored Syrian-born poet and essayist; and the selected poems of the Greek poet Kiki Dimoula. Already recruited as consulting editors are the Italian medievalist, semiotician, and novelist Umberto Eco; the fifteenth poet laureate of the United States, Charles Simic; Nobel Prize–winning novelist Orhan Pamuk of Turkey; and Nobel laureate Elie Wiesel.

"Part of what drives this for me is the knowledge that just 2 percent of what gets published in the United States today is work in translation," Donatich said. "The great ambition of this series is to help reverse the trend against literary translations, a kind of virtual censorship that further insulates our culture. It also gives Yale University Press another way to contribute something tangible to a world culture. For me, it is the fulfillment of a career dream and one whose legacy I hope will outlive me." Another new project he was pleased to announce was formation of Jewish Lives, a series of contemporary biographies to be published in partnership with the Leon D. Black Foundation and which, like the Why X Matters concept, will pair interesting authors with interesting subjects. Forthcoming titles include *Kafka*, by Saul Friedlander; *Sarah Bernhardt*, by Robert Gottlieb; *Disraeli*, by David Cesarani; *Dylan*, by Ron Rosenbaum; and *Rashi* by Jack Miles.

Another top goal, said Donatich, is one that will allow the Press to control and provide access to what he called "our legacy content"—another way of saying "all the books published in our first century"—through a "diverse and widening series of digital media outlets." A related undertaking is the creation of a platform that will allow the Press to have its own electronic publishing imprint. "The Stalin Archive is the cornerstone of this project," he said, "but it will also provide an ideal home for the Anchor Yale Bible program, a scholarly edition of the classic in several hundred volumes which the Press bought from Doubleday in 2007. It will also host digital and multimedia value-added publication of a medieval manuscript project, bilingual editions of Margellos translations, a digital poetry archive with 'live readings,' and even, someday, an interactive blog of real-time scholarship."

Donatich said that while he spends a good deal of his time "defending the beautiful and irreplaceable convention of the printed book," he welcomes the prospect of offering the Press as "a kind of digital research center" that before long will be commissioning electronic editions of primary documents that invite scholarly discovery and commentary. "The capacity to provide an online digital concordance to the Bible, or an online access to a fragile medieval manuscript complete with commentary, pedagogy, telescoping illumination, and musical examples to just about anyone who wants it gives me goosebumps," he said. "It's exciting to imagine the discovery of new communication technologies that will enable innovative research and teaching skills, and to be among the pioneers in implementing them. I see these events as consistent with our mission, and can think of no better way to build on what the Press has stood for and accomplished over the past hundred years."

Notes

Quotations and information drawn from the minutes of meetings kept by the Publications Committee, Governing Board, and Finance Committee of Yale University Press are identified by date in the body of the text; copies of these proceedings are maintained in the office of the director. Interviews conducted by the author are clearly identified as such in the text; all were recorded and transcribed by the author.

Preface

x *University Publishing in a Digital Age,* also known as the *Ithaka Report,* by Laura Brown, Rebecca Griffiths, and Matthew Rascoff, with a preface by Kevin Guthrie, sponsored financially by Ithaka and JSTOR, an online archive of scholarly journals; the full text of the report is available free of charge at ithaka.org. For an excellent overview of what many perceive as a "crisis" in scholarly publishing, see Peter Givler, "University Press Publishing in the United States," in *Scholarly Publishing: Books, Journals, Publishers, and Libraries in the Twentieth Century,* ed. Richard E. Abel and Lyman W. Newlin (New York: Wiley, 2001), 107–120. For a more complete perspective, see also Will Nixon, "University Presses: Highs and Lows," *Publishers Weekly,* September 22, 1989, 20; Eric Bryant, "Reinventing the University Press," *Library Journal,* September 1, 1994, 147–149; Phil Pochoda, "Universities Press On," *Nation,*

December 29, 1997, 11–16; Karen J. Winkler, "Academic Presses Look to the Internet to Save Scholarly Monographs," *Chronicle of Higher Education,* September 12, 1997, A18; and Christopher Shea, "A Small, Respected University Press Fights Off a Push to Eliminate It: Arkansas Debate Highlights the Economic Difficulties of Academic Publishing," *Chronicle of Higher Education,* April 17, 1998, A16–A17.

Chapter 1: The Formative Decades

1   For the history and background of Oxford University Press, see Nicolas Barker, *The Oxford University Press and the Spread of Learning* (Oxford: Clarendon Press, 1978); for Cambridge University Press, see David McKitterick, *A History of Cambridge University Press,* 3 vols. (Cambridge: Cambridge University Press, 1992–2002).

3   For more on the history of American university presses, see John Tebbel, *A History of Book Publishing in the United States,* 4 vols. (New York: R. R. Bowker, 1972–1981); Gene R. Hawes, *To Advance Knowledge: A Handbook on American University Press Publishing* (New York: Association of American University Presses, 1967); and Chester Kerr, *A Report on American University Presses,* hereafter referred to as the *Kerr Report* (New York: Association of American University Presses, 1949). For more on Daniel Coit Gilman, see Abraham Flexner, *Daniel Coit Gilman: Creator of the American Type of University* (New York: Harcourt, Brace, 1946); and Albert Muto, *The University of California Press: The Early Years, 1893–1953* (Berkeley: University of California Press, 1992). For more on William Rainey Harper, see Thomas Wakefield Goodspeed, *William Rainey Harper: First President of the University of Chicago* (Chicago: University of Chicago Press, 1928). For more on Nicholas Murray Butler, see Michael Rosenthal, *Nicholas Miraculous: The Amazing Career of the Redoubtable Dr. Nicholas Murray Butler* (New York: Farrar, Straus and Giroux, 2006). For more on Princeton University Press, see James Axtell, *The Making*

of Princeton University (Princeton: Princeton University Press, 2006), 530–592. The first formal use of the phrase "university press" in the United States was at Cornell in 1869, but that enterprise, according to the *Kerr Report,* was "found wanting" and was discontinued in 1884. Harvard—the first college to be established in North America—did not open its own publishing operation until 1913, though the first printing press to be set up in British North America was established by Stephen Daye in 1638 in the house of Henry Dunster, the founding president of Harvard College.

7   "our best products": Quoted in George Parmly Day, *Yale University Press: 1908–1920* (New Haven: Yale University Press, 1920), 12. Copy located in Yns511, Manuscripts and Archives, Sterling Memorial Library, Yale University.

9   "Mr. Eisenman": From notes of a conversation with Alvin Eisenman, MS 1566, Roberta Yerkes Blanshard, box 2, folder 33, Beinecke Rare Book and Manuscript Library, Yale University.

9   Clarence Day's essay, "The Story of the Yale University Press Told by a Friend," was reprinted in Chester Kerr's *Some Not Unbiased Notes and Footnotes on the First Seventy-Five Years of the Yale University Press, 1908–1983,* a commemorative pamphlet printed by Yale University Press in 1983, hereafter cited as *Seventy-Five.* John Tebbel writes that George Parmly Day "provided the initial capital stock of nearly a quarter million dollars" to establish Yale University Press and "raised enough money to establish a substantial endowment fund, as well as a building to house the press" (*History of Book Publishing,* 2:539).

11   Carl Purington Rollins: "recover the technique," quoted in Tebbel, *History of Book Publishing,* 3:348; "excellent designer," quoted in Joseph Blumenthal, *The Printed Book in America* (Boston: David R. Godine, 1977), 41. For a discussion of Rollins and his contributions to American bookmaking, see also Megan Benton, *Beauty and the Book: Fine Editions and Cultural Distinction in America* (New Haven and London: Yale University Press, 2000). See also *The Work of Carl Purington*

Rollins, catalogue of an exhibit at the Grolier Club, arranged by the American Institute of Graphic Arts, April 27, 1949.

13   "significant of the vision": George Parmly Day, *The New Era of Publishing at Yale: Being an Address Delivered on Alumni Day, February Twenty-Third, Nineteen Hundred and Fourteen* (New Haven: Yale University Press, 1914), 4. Copy located in Yns511, Manuscripts and Archives, Sterling Memorial Library, Yale University.

13   "did not testify": Ibid., 8.

15   For more on Wilmarth Lewis, see Wilmarth S. Lewis, *Collector's Progress* (New York: Alfred A. Knopf, 1951); and Nicholas A. Basbanes, *A Gentle Madness: Bibliophiles, Bibliomanes, and the Eternal Passion for Books* (New York: Holt, 1995), 23–24.

16   "it was something": Mel Gussow, "Warren Smith, 93; Edited Walpole's Letters," *New York Times,* November 26, 1998.

19   Scroll and Key: George Parmly Day reports the fifty-thousand-dollar gift from the Kingsley Trust Association in *Yale University Press: 1908–1920,* 8.

23   Chronicles of America Photoplays: The full text of George Parmly Day's announcement was published in the *New York Times* on September 28, 1923. Copies of documents pertaining to Chronicles of America Picture Corp. are filed with the minutes maintained of Press board meetings in vol. 5, titled "The Chronicles of America Picture Corporation Minute Book." For a comprehensive discussion of Yale's venture into filmmaking, see Donald J. Mattheisen, "Filming U.S. History during the 1920s: The Chronicles of America Photoplays," *Historian* 54 (1992): 626–640; and Ian Tyrrell, *Historians in Public: The Practice of American History* (Chicago: University of Chicago Press, 2005), 78–81. See also Paul Saettler, *The Evolution of American Educational Technology* (Englewood, CO: Libraries Unlimited, 1990), 102–103; and Charles Francis Hoban and Edward Bunn Van Ormer, *Instructional Film Research, 1918–1950,* issued in 1951 as Technical report no. SDC 269-7-19 of the Instructional Film Research Program, Pennsylvania State College.

24 "scholars in all matters": Quoted in Mattheisen, "Filming U.S. History," 631.

24 "guiding light": Tyrrell, *Historians in Public*, 78.

24 "Must we conclude": Quoted in Mattheisen, "Filming U.S. History," 632.

25 "word spread": Ibid., 630.

25 "What sort of fences": *Metropolitan Museum of Art Bulletin*, 20, no. 7 (1925): 186–187.

26 "was found financially": *Time*, August 2, 1926.

26 "Despite the admitted excellence": Quoted in Mattheisen, "Filming U.S. History," 638.

27 "That the photoplays": Daniel Chauncey Knowlton and John Warren Tilton, *Motion Pictures in History Teaching: A Study of the Chronicles of America Photoplays, as an Aid in Seventh Grade Instruction* (New Haven: Yale University Press, 1929), 93.

28 Yale Series of Younger Poets: See George Bradley, ed., *The Yale Younger Poets Anthology* (New Haven and London: Yale University Press, 1998); and Ted Olson, "Speaking of Books: The Yale Younger Poets," *New York Times*, January 26, 1970.

29 "rare work of scholarship": Peter Gay, "Carl Becker's Heavenly City," *Political Science Quarterly* 72, no. 2 (1957): 182.

31 "I propose to take": William Osler, *The Evolution of Modern Medicine* (New Haven: Yale University Press, 1921), 6.

32 "Eventually, we reach": Edwin Hubble, *The Realm of the Nebulae* (New Haven: Yale University Press, 1936), 202.

33 "For his prime tool": "Babies," *Time*, September 24, 1934.

34 "For Heidegger": Ralph Manheim, in Martin Heidegger, *An Introduction to Metaphysics* (New Haven: Yale University Press, 1959), vii.

35 "The works that are being peddled": Heidegger, *Introduction to Metaphysics*, 199. For more on the long-standing relationship between Heidegger and Hannah Arendt, see Elżbieta Ettinger, *Hannah Arendt/Martin Heidegger* (New Haven and London: Yale University Press, 1995). After World War II, Ettinger asserts, Arendt became Heidegger's "devoted if unpaid agent in the United States, finding publishers, negotiating

contracts, and selecting the best translators. Above all, she did what she could to whitewash his Nazi past" (78). Why she did not persuade Heidegger to delete this egregious statement of support for his old political affiliation in the American edition of this book, however, remains a mystery.

35   "university presses are allowed": *New York Times,* June 11, 1978.

38   "Our study": Riesman quoted in *Citation Classics,* July 28, 1980.

40   "With unerring hindsight": Todd Gitlin, foreword to David Riesman, *The Lonely Crowd* (New Haven and London: Yale Nota Bene, 2001), xii–xiv.

41   "the most beautiful man": Bennett Cerf, *At Random: The Reminiscences of Bennett Cerf* (New York: Random House, 1977), 81.

42   "When O'Neill gave us": Arthur and Barbara Gelb, *O'Neill* (New York: Harper and Row, 1962), 862.

42   "We put the manuscript": Cerf, *At Random,* 89.

43   "been assured": Letter to the editor, *New York Times,* March 11, 1956.

47   "When some of his activities": *Seventy-Five,* 2.

50   *ABC of Reading:* In a letter dated March 25, 1949 (carbon copy located in the contract files for "E. Pound"), Norman V. Donaldson, managing director of the Press, advised Dorothy Pound that *ABC of Reading* "has been out of print since January 1941 and therefore no royalties have been earned on that title. We do not plan to reprint it so the rights to the book revert to the author." He further reported that $26.32 royalties were due on *Make It New.* I thank Peggy Fox, president and publisher of New Directions, for information on the subsequent publishing history of *ABC of Reading* and *Make It New.*

51   "angry convert . . . betrayer of his country": *New York Times,* March 14, 1946.

51   Reaction from Pound's lawyer: See Robert A. Corrigan, "What's My Line? Bennett Cerf, Ezra Pound and the American Poet," *American Quarterly* 24 (1972): 101–113.

52 "It never bothered me": Linda Kuehl, "Talk with James Laughlin: New and Old Directions," *New York Times,* February 25, 1973.

52 "an admiration": Harvey Breit, "Repeat Performances," *New York Times,* June 3, 1951.

53 "consternation": *Kerr Report,* 3.

56 "David Dallin's *Soviet Espionage*": John Earl Haynes and Harvey Klehr, "International Communism and Espionage" session, European Social Science History Conference, March 2006, Amsterdam.

57 "some new things . . . over and over again": Eugene Davidson, *Reflections on a Disruptive Decade: Essays on the Sixties* (Columbia: University of Missouri Press, 2000), 3–5.

59 "I come now": John Kenneth Galbraith, "In Defense of Laissez-Faire," *New York Times,* October 30, 1949.

60 "merely attempts": Letter to the editor, *New York Times,* December 11, 1949.

61 "I have been driven": Quoted in "Charles A. Beard, Historian, Is Dead," *New York Times,* September 2, 1948. See also James P. Philbin, "Charles Austin Beard: Liberal Foe of American Internationalism," *Humanitas* 13, no. 2 (2000). 90–107.

62 "Lewis Mumford, the writer": "Beard, Historian, Is Dead."

64 "unfavorably received": Harold E. Williamson and Ralph Louis Andreano, "Integration and Competition in the Oil Industry," *Journal of Political Economy* 69 (1961): 381–385.

64 "four professional economists . . . and the Press": Ralph Cassady, Jr., *Price Making and Price Behavior in the Petroleum Industry,* Petroleum Monograph Series, vol. 1 (New Haven: Yale University Press, 1954), ix–x.

67 "cultivate the resources": *Articles of Government as Adopted by the Board of Governors and the Yale Corporation, March–April 1961, and Amended by the Board and the Corporation, May–June 1978,* 1.

68 "The PC . . . made it fun": John G. Ryden, "What Would Ralph Say?" *Yale Law Journal* 108 (1999): 1479–1481.

Chapter 2: The Middle Years

72   "Some were very specific": *Kerr Report,* 12.
72   "The function of a university press": Quoted in *Kerr Report,*
       12.
73   "Our American university presses": Ibid., 267.
73   "the third function": Quoted in William H. Honan, "Chester
       Brooks Kerr, 86, Scholars' Editor," *New York Times,* August
       26, 1999.
74   "Over a period of years . . . techniques of publishing": *Kerr
       Report,* 263.
75   "By the time . . . scholarly publishing": Ibid., 4–7.
77   "stylish, scholarly": *AAP Newsletter,* December 6, 1976, quoted
       in John Tebbel, *A History of Book Publishing in the United
       States,* 4 vols. (New York: R. R. Bowker, 1972–1981), 4:635.
81   The Vinland Map: For a comprehensive overview of this epi-
       sode, see "The Case of the Vinland Map," in the second edi-
       tion of *The Vinland Map and the Tartar Relation* (New Haven
       and London: Yale University Press, 1995), xxi–xxvii.
82   "the most exciting single acquisition": *New York Times,* Oc-
       tober 11, 1965.
83   "against the wall": *New York Times,* November 25, 1965.
84   "We planned to publish": Quoted in "Scholarly Publishing:
       'Madness with a Method,'" *Yale Alumni Magazine,* April 1968,
       16–23.
88   Josef Albers: For more on Albers and his work, see Rob Roy
       Kelly, "The Early Years of Graphic Design at Yale University,"
       Design Issues 17, no. 3 (2001): 3–14; also Irving Sandler, "The
       School of Art at Yale, 1950–1970: The Collective Reminis-
       cences of Twenty Distinguished Alumni," *Art Journal* 42, no.
       1 (1982): 14–21.
91   "the famous Vinland Map": *New York Times,* January 26, 1974.
92   "To the extent possible": Quoted in Jennifer Kaylin, "Tales
       of the 'Un-Fake,'" *Yale Alumni Magazine,* May 1996. For a
       thorough discussion of the controversy surrounding the Vin-
       land Map, see Kirsten A. Seaver, *Maps, Myths, and Men: The*

Story of the Vinland Map (Stanford, CA: Stanford University Press, 2004).

94   "noted for his interest": Robin W. Winks, *Cloak and Gown: Scholars in the Secret War, 1939–1961* (New Haven and London: Yale University Press, 1996), 292.

95   "instant classic": Ibid., 296.

95   "As the secrets of the war": J. C. Masterman, *The Double-Cross System in the War of 1939 to 1945* (New Haven and London: Yale University Press, 1972), xvi.

96   "At Yale I was removed": Marilyn Frankel, "Venerable Boston Book Publisher Reborn in New Haven," *New York Times,* October 12, 1980.

96   Professional affiliations: Chester Kerr served as president of the Association of American University Presses from 1965 to 1967 and as a consultant to the Ford Foundation's publishing programs from 1975 to 1978.

105   Paul Mellon: To commemorate the centennial of Paul Mellon's birth in 2007 and to accompany an exhibition that traveled from the Yale Center for British Art in New Haven to the Royal Academy of Arts in London, the Press published *Paul Mellon's Legacy: A Passion for British Art,* an elegant book filled with 370 color illustrations and featuring essays by John Baskett, Jules David Prown, Duncan Robinson, Brian Allen, and William Reese.

105   The Yale book on William Hogarth published for the Paul Mellon Centre for Studies in British Art: Ronald Paulson, *Hogarth: His Life, Art, and Times,* 2 vols. (New Haven and London: Yale University Press, 1971).

109   "the job of a university press": It was Thomas James Wilson, director of Harvard University Press from 1946 to 1967, who famously said, "A university press exists to publish as many good scholarly books as possible short of bankruptcy." The statement has appeared variously in the *Kerr Report,* 13, *Publishers Weekly,* April 22, 1963, and Max Hall, *Harvard University Press: A History* (Cambridge, MA: Harvard University Press, 1986), 125.

114   Yale winners of the Eric Mitchell Prize, administered by *Burlington Magazine* of London: Colin B. Bailey, *Patriotic Taste: Collecting Modern Art in Pre-Revolutionary Paris* (2002); David Anfam, *Mark Rothko: The Works on Canvas* (1998); Kathleen A. Foster, *Thomas Eakins Rediscovered* (1998); David Bindman and Malcolm Baker, *Roubiliac and the Eighteenth-Century Monument: Sculpture as Theatre* (1995); David Landau and Peter Parshall, *The Renaissance Print, 1470–1550* (1994); Jennifer Montagu, *Alessandro Algardi* (1985); Graham Reynolds, *The Later Paintings and Drawings of John Constable* (1984); Michael Baxandall, *The Limewood Sculptors of Renaissance Germany* (1980); and Martin Butlin and Evelyn Joll, *The Paintings of J. M. W. Turner* (1977). Mitchell Prizes given in recognition of an outstanding "first book" by an author: Andrew Butterfield, *The Sculptures of Andrea del Verrocchio* (1997); Patricia Lee Rubin, *Giorgio Vasari: Art and History* (1995); David Franklin, *Rosso in Italy: The Italian Career of Rosso Fiorentino* (1994); William Hood, *Fra Angelico at San Marco* (1993); Clare Robertson, *"Il Gran Cardinale": Alessandro Farnese, Patron of the Arts* (1992); Peter Galassi, *Corot in Italy* (1992); Cecilia Powell, *Turner in the South: Rome, Naples, Florence* (1987); and Thomas E. Crow, *Painters and Public Life in Eighteenth Century Paris* (1985).

118   "It is a remarkable book": Edward Rothstein, "A History for Kids That Isn't Child's Play," *New York Times,* October 3, 2005.

119   "works of scholarship": Quoted in Honan, "Chester Brooks Kerr."

Chapter 3: Enriching the Mix

122   Combined Press revenues: Of the $30,752,000 reported for fiscal 2007, New Haven sales accounted for $23,061,000, London $7,691,000.

125   "I think it is horrendous . . . academic monograph": Quoted in Nicholas A. Basbanes, *Patience and Fortitude* (New York: HarperCollins, 2001), 436–439.

125 "lost its soul": Leon F. Litwack, "Has the Library Lost Its Soul?" *California Monthly* 108 (February 1998).

126 "Our experience so far": Quoted in Basbanes, *Patience and Fortitude,* 440, and reaffirmed when contacted by the author again in the summer of 2007.

127 "the acquisitions budgets": Ibid., 429.

127 "Federal funding for higher education": The National Defense Education Act (NDEA) of 1958 was enacted into law a year after the Soviet Union launched Sputnik and was intended primarily to stimulate the advancement of education in science, mathematics, and modern foreign languages. It also provided financial support for technical education, area studies, geography, English as a second language, counseling and guidance, the building of school libraries, the acquisition of educational media, and the training of librarians. The NDEA was supplemented in 1965 by the Higher Education Act. Funding for the program ended in 1972.

128 "There has been an argument": Ibid., 463.

136 "the opportunity to write the book": Quoted in Michael Luzzi, "New Book Studies Jesus' Impact on Culture," *New York Times,* December 1, 1985.

137 "Whereas we as the Yale University faculty": Jaroslav Pelikan, *The University's Secret Weapon* (New Haven: Friends of Yale University Press, 1992), 6–7.

141 "a happy day": John Russell, "Art," *New York Times,* December 3, 1995.

145 "the most imaginative and wide-ranging editor": Quoted in Nick Ravo, "Edward Tripp, 79, Creator of New York Encyclopedia, Dies," *New York Times,* April 9, 1999.

153 "Everything that was ever suspected": Christopher Hitchens, book review of *Spain Betrayed: The Soviet Union in the Spanish Civil War, Wilson Quarterly* 25, no. 3 (2001): 106.

153 "If Spain were Vietnam": Sam Tanenhaus, "Innocents Abroad," *Vanity Fair,* September 2001, 286.

155 "secrecy system": Daniel Patrick Moynihan, *Secrecy: The*

American Experience (New Haven and London: Yale University Press, 1998), 15.

156   "If you have influence": William F. Buckley, Jr., "Read All about It! But Hurry," *National Review,* April 22, 1996.

158   Chicago bookseller: See Stuart Brent, *The Seven Stairs* (Boston: Houghton Mifflin, 1962).

159   Annals of Communism response: The political reaction to the Annals of Communism has followed predictable lines and need not be discussed in detail here. For a sampling of the conflicting views that have been expressed, see Eric Alterman, "A Cold War over the Cold War? Yale University Press's Annals of Communism Book Series Attacked from All Sides," *Nation,* February 15, 1999; and John J. Miller, "The Annals of Jonathan Brent: One Man and a Great Publishing Project," *National Review,* May 22, 2006.

160   Culture and Civilization of China: See Bill Slocum, "China, the Oldest Culture, in Mega-Tomes," *New York Times,* January 4, 1998; Scott Heller, "Yale Press Starts Mammoth Book Project on Chinese Culture: Scholars from U.S. and China Will Collaborate on 75 Volumes," *Chronicle of Higher Education,* November 14, 1997.

165   "Over the years": Richard Levin, to the Yale University Press Community, March 28, 2002, from office files.

Chapter 4: A Press in Transition

170   "a set of criteria": See David A. Bell, "The Bookless Future: What the Internet Is Doing to Scholarship," *New Republic,* May 2, 2005, 27.

Centennial Highlights

This list includes some of the many best-selling, prize-winning, and seminal works published by Yale University Press since 1908. Each title is listed under the year in which it was originally published by the Press. For a complete list of prize-winning titles, visit the Press Web site at yalebooks .com/awards.

1913
The Framing of the Constitution of the United States
MAX FARRAND

1921
The Nature of the Judicial Process
BENJAMIN N. CARDOZO

1922
An Introduction to the Philosophy of Law
ROSCOE POUND

1934
The Colonial Period of American History: The Settlements, Volume 1
CHARLES M. ANDREWS
Winner of the 1935 Pulitzer Prize in History

A Common Faith
JOHN DEWEY

1938
Psychology and Religion
CARL GUSTAV JUNG

1940
*Daily Life in Ancient Rome: The People and the City at the
Height of the Empire*
JÉRÔME CARCOPINO; edited and annotated by HENRY T.
ROSWELL; translated by E. O. LORIMER

1941
God and Philosophy
ÉTIENNE GILSON

1944
*An Essay on Man: An Introduction to a Philosophy of Human
Culture*
ERNST CASSIRER

1949
*The Meaning of Evolution: A Study of the History of Life and
of Its Significance for Man*
GEORGE GAYLORD SIMPSON

1950
*The American Mind: An Interpretation of American Thought and
Character since the 1880's*
HENRY STEELE COMMAGER

Psychoanalysis and Religion
ERICH FROMM

The Lonely Crowd: A Study of the Changing American Character
DAVID RIESMAN in collaboration with REUEL DENNEY and
NATHAN GLAZER

1952
The Courage to Be
PAUL TILLICH

1953
The Making of the Middle Ages
R. W. SOUTHERN

1954
Way to Wisdom: An Introduction to Philosophy
KARL JASPERS; translated by RALPH MANHEIM

1955
Becoming: Basic Considerations for a Psychology of Personality
GORDON W. ALLPORT

*The Shingle Style and the Stick Style: Architectural Theory and Design
from Richardson to the Origins of Wright*
VINCENT J. SCULLY, JR.

1956
On Painting
LEON BATTISTA ALBERTI; translated with introduction
and notes by JOHN R. SPENCER

Long Day's Journey into Night
EUGENE O'NEILL
Winner of the 1957 Pulitzer Prize in Drama

1958
The Computer and the Brain
JOHN VON NEUMANN

1961
Who Governs? Democracy and Power in an American City
ROBERT A. DAHL

Poems
ALAN DUGAN
Winner of the 1962 Pulitzer Prize and National Book Award
in Poetry

1962
Mankind Evolving: The Evolution of the Human Species
THEODOSIUS DOBZHANSKY

Beginning Japanese: Part 1
ELEANOR HARZ JORDEN and HAMAKO ITO CHAPLIN

The Shape of Time: Remarks on the History of Things
GEORGE KUBLER

1964
The Autobiography of Benjamin Franklin
BENJAMIN FRANKLIN; edited by LEONARD W. LABAREE,
RALPH L. KETCHAM, HELEN C. BOATFIELD, and
HELENE H. FINEMAN

The Morality of Law
LON L. FULLER

1965
Man Adapting
RENÉ DUBOS

1966
Arms and Influence
THOMAS C. SCHELLING

1967
Wilderness and the American Mind
RODERICK NASH

Pigs for the Ancestors: Ritual in the Ecology of a New Guinea People
ROY A. RAPPAPORT

1968
Political Order in Changing Societies
SAMUEL P. HUNTINGTON

1971
Interaction of Color
Text of the original edition with selected plates
JOSEF ALBERS

1972
A Religious History of the American People
SYDNEY E. AHLSTROM
Winner of the 1973 National Book Award in
Philosophy/Religion

*The Children of Pride: Selected Letters of the Family of the
Rev. Dr. Charles Colcock Jones from the Years 1860–1868*
ROBERT MANSON MYERS
Winner of the 1973 National Book Award in History

1973
The Formation of Islamic Art
OLEG GRABAR

Field Guide
ROBERT HASS
Yale Series of Younger Poets

1974
Congress: The Electoral Connection
DAVID R. MAYHEW

1977
The Bonds of Womanhood: "Woman's Sphere" in New England,
1780–1835
NANCY F. COTT

1978
The Origins of Knowledge and Imagination
JACOB BRONOWSKI; foreword by S. E. LURIA

Life in the English Country House: A Social and Architectural History
MARK GIROUARD

1979
The Madwoman in the Attic: The Woman Writer and the
Nineteenth-Century Literary Imagination
SANDRA M. GILBERT and SUSAN GUBAR

Sexual Harassment of Working Women: A Case of Sex Discrimination
CATHARINE A. MACKINNON; foreword by THOMAS I.
EMERSON

1980
The Limewood Sculptors of Renaissance Germany
MICHAEL BAXANDALL

Patrons and Painters: A Study in the Relations between Italian Art
and Society in the Age of the Baroque, Revised and enlarged edition
FRANCIS HASKELL

1981
The Paintings and Drawings of William Blake
MARTIN BUTLIN
Published for the Paul Mellon Centre for Studies in
British Art

Mary Chesnut's Civil War
MARY CHESNUT; edited by C. VANN WOODWARD
Winner of the 1982 Pulitzer Prize in History

Rhyme's Reason: A Guide to English Verse
JOHN HOLLANDER

Roots of Revolution: An Interpretive History of Modern Iran
NIKKI R. KEDDIE; with a section by YANN RICHARD
(The current edition is titled *Modern Iran: Roots and
Results of Revolution*)

1982
*The Rise and Decline of Nations: Economic Growth,
Stagflation, and Social Rigidities*
MANCUR OLSON

1983
The First Urban Christians: The Social World of the Apostle Paul
WAYNE A. MEEKS

1984
The Chronicle of the Lodz Ghetto, 1941–1944
LUCJAN DOBROSZYCKI

Chivalry
MAURICE KEEN

1985
Painters and Public Life in Eighteenth-Century Paris
THOMAS E. CROW

The Treasure Houses of Britain: Five Hundred Years of Private Patronage and Art Collecting
Edited by GERVASE JACKSON-STOPS
Copublished with the National Gallery of Art, Washington

Jesus through the Centuries: His Place in the History of Culture
JAROSLAV PELIKAN

Paul Rand: A Designer's Art
PAUL RAND

1986
Art and Beauty in the Middle Ages
UMBERTO ECO; translated by HUGH BREDIN

Monet: Nature into Art
JOHN HOUSE

The Shaping of America: A Geographical Perspective on 500 Years of History
Volume 1: *Atlantic America, 1492–1800*
D. W. MEINIG

1987
French in Action: A Beginning Course in Language and Culture
PIERRE CAPRETZ; with contributions by BÉATRICE ABETTI and MARIE-ODILE GERMAIN; foreword by LAURENCE WYLIE

1988
Impressionism: Art, Leisure, and Parisian Society
ROBERT L. HERBERT

1989
Monet in the '90s: The Series Paintings
PAUL HAYES TUCKER

1990
Sexual Personae: Art and Decadence from Nefertiti to Emily Dickinson
CAMILLE PAGLIA

A History of South Africa
LEONARD THOMPSON

1991
Holocaust Testimonies: The Ruins of Memory
LAWRENCE L. LANGER
Winner of the 1991 National Book Critics Circle Award in Criticism

1992
Britons: Forging the Nation, 1707–1837
LINDA COLLEY

The Stripping of the Altars: Traditional Religion in England, c. 1400–c. 1580
EAMON DUFFY

1993
Opera in America: A Cultural History
JOHN DIZIKES
Winner of the 1993 National Book Critics Circle Award in Criticism

1995
The Encyclopedia of New York City
Edited by KENNETH T. JACKSON
Copublished with the New-York Historical Society

The Secret World of American Communism
    HARVEY KLEHR, JOHN EARL HAYNES, and FRIDRIKH
    IGOREVICH FIRSOV; Russian documents translated by
    TIMOTHY D. SERGAY
    Annals of Communism series

    1996
Thomas Cranmer: A Life
    DIARMAID MACCULLOCH

    1998
Belief in God in an Age of Science
    JOHN POLKINGHORNE

*Seeing Like a State: How Certain Schemes to Improve the
Human Condition Have Failed*
    JAMES C. SCOTT

The Gentleman's Daughter: Women's Lives in Georgian England
    AMANDA VICKERY

    1999
*Unearthing the Past: Archaeology and Aesthetics in the Making of
Renaissance Culture*
    LEONARD BARKAN

Farewell to an Idea: Episodes from a History of Modernism
    T. J. CLARK

Five Days in London, May 1940
    JOHN LUKACS

Web Style Guide: Basic Design Principles for Creating Web Sites
    PATRICK J. LYNCH and SARAH HORTON

2000
Introduction to Metaphysics
MARTIN HEIDEGGER; new translation by GREGORY FRIED
and RICHARD POLT

Taliban: Militant Islam, Oil and Fundamentalism in Central Asia
AHMED RASHID

2001
Lichens of North America
IRWIN M. BRODO, SYLVIA DURAN SHARNOFF, and
STEPHEN SHARNOFF; with selected drawings by
SUSAN LAURIE-BOURQUE; foreword by PETER RAVEN
Published in collaboration with the Canadian Museum
of Nature

*Narrative of the Life of Frederick Douglass, an American Slave:
Written by Himself*
FREDERICK DOUGLASS; edited by JOHN W. BLASSINGAME,
JOHN R. MCKIVIGAN, and PETER P. HINKS; GERALD
FULKERSON, textual editor; JAMES H. COOK, VICTORIA C.
GRUBER, and C. JANE HOLTAN, editorial assistants

The Holocaust Encyclopedia
Edited by WALTER LAQUEUR; JUDITH TYDOR BAUMEL,
associate editor

Utopia
THOMAS MORE; a new translation with an introduction
by CLARENCE H. MILLER

2002
Benjamin Franklin
EDMUND S. MORGAN

One World: The Ethics of Globalization
PETER SINGER

2003
Jonathan Edwards: A Life
GEORGE M. MARSDEN
Winner of the 2004 Bancroft Prize

Inventing a Nation: Washington, Adams, Jefferson
GORE VIDAL

The Spirit of Early Christian Thought: Seeking the Face of God
ROBERT LOUIS WILKEN

2004
The Artist's Reality: Philosophies of Art
MARK ROTHKO; edited and with an introduction by
CHRISTOPHER ROTHKO

American Judaism: A History
JONATHAN D. SARNA

Red Sky at Morning: America and the Crisis of the Global Environment
JAMES GUSTAVE SPETH

Why Globalization Works
MARTIN WOLF

2005
Dwelling Place: A Plantation Epic
ERSKINE CLARKE
Winner of the 2006 Bancroft Prize

A Little History of the World
  E. H. GOMBRICH; translated by CAROLINE MUSTILL;
  illustrated by CLIFFORD HARPER

2006
*Empires of the Atlantic World: Britain and Spain in America,
1492–1830*
  J. H. ELLIOTT
  Winner of the 2007 Francis Parkman Prize
  awarded by the Society of American Historians

The Yale Book of Quotations
  Edited by FRED R. SHAPIRO; foreword by JOSEPH EPSTEIN

2007
Stuart Davis: A Catalogue Raisonné
  Edited by ANI BOYAJIAN and MARK RUTKOSKI;
  with essays by WILLIAM C. AGEE and KAREN WILKIN
  Published in association with the Yale University
  Art Gallery

Stanley: The Impossible Life of Africa's Greatest Explorer
  TIM JEAL
  Winner of the 2007 National Book Critics Circle Award
  in Biography

Series, Editions, and Museum Publishing Partners

Among the distinguished *scholarly editions* published by the
Press since 1908 are The Yale Edition of Horace Walpole's Corre-
spondence (first volume published 1937); Yale Judaica Series (1948);
The Works of Jonathan Edwards (1957); The Yale Edition of the
Works of Samuel Johnson (1958); The Papers of Benjamin Franklin
(1959); Complete Prose Works of John Milton (1953); The Yale Edi-
tion of the Complete Works of St. Thomas More (1963); and The
Frederick Douglass Papers (1982).

The publishing program also includes dozens of *series*. Here is a selection of some of the oldest, newest, and best known: Yale Studies in English (first volume published in 1908); Storrs Lectures (1911); Silliman Memorial Lectures on Science (1912); The Yale Shakespeare (1917); Chronicles of America (1919); Yale Series of Younger Poets (1919); Terry Lectures (1925); Yale Publications in the History of Art (1939); Yale Paperbounds (1959); Lamar Series in Western History (formerly the Yale Western Americana series, 1962); Yale Fastbacks (1970); The Psychoanalytic Study of the Child (1976); Yale University Press Pelican History of Art (1988); Rethinking the Western Tradition (1994); Annals of Communism (1995); Pevsner Architectural Guides (1995); The Culture & Civilization of China (1997); Icons of America (2003); Annotated Shakespeare (2003); Yale University Press Health & Wellness (2004); Why X Matters (2006); Anchor Yale Bible (2008); Cecile and Theodore Margellos World Republic of Letters (2008); The Yale Drama Series (2008). For more information about series and editions, visit the Series and Editions section of the Press's Web site (yalebooks.com).

The list has also been graced with important and beautiful books published in cooperation with distinguished *museums*. As of 2008, the Press's exclusive publishing partners include Addison Gallery of American Art; The Art Institute of Chicago; Bard Graduate Center; The Sterling and Francine Clark Art Institute; Dallas Museum of Art; Harvard University Art Museums; The Japan Society; The Jewish Museum; Kimbell Art Museum; The Menil Collection; The Museum of Fine Arts, Houston; The Metropolitan Museum of Art; National Gallery, London; National Gallery of Art, Center for Advanced Study in the Visual Arts; Paul Mellon Centre for Studies in British Art; Philadelphia Museum of Art; Princeton University Art Museum; Whitney Museum of American Art; Yale Center for British Art; and Yale University Art Gallery. For more information about the Press's museum publications and publishing partners, visit the Web site at yalebooks.com/art.